T0195708

ULTIMATE PRAISE

PSALMS: PRAISING GOD IN ALL CIRCUMSTANCES

INYANG UKOT

WESTBOW
PRESS®
A DIVISION OF THOMAS NELSON
& ZONDERVAN

WestBow Press books may be ordered through booksellers or by contacting:

WestBow Press
A Division of Thomas Nelson & Zondervan
1663 Liberty Drive
Bloomington, IN 47403
www.westbowpress.com
1 (866) 928-1240

Unless marked otherwise, all Scripture quotations are taken from The Holy Bible, New International Version®, NIV® Copyright © 1973, 1978, 1984, 2011 by Biblica, Inc.® Used by permission. All rights reserved worldwide.

Scripture quotations marked NKJV are taken from the New King James Version®. Copyright © 1982 by Thomas Nelson. Used by permission. All rights reserved.

Scripture quotations marked KJV are taken from the King James Version.

ISBN: 978-1-9736-8880-8 (sc)
ISBN: 978-1-9736-8879-2 (hc)
ISBN: 978-1-9736-8881-5 (e)

Library of Congress Control Number: 2020905183

Print information available on the last page.

WestBow Press rev. date: 4/22/2020

TABLE OF CONTENTS

DEDICATION

This book is dedicated to the children, young people, adults and elderly who have chosen to be students of the Bible, using all available tools – including this very mind- and spirit-stimulating 'life-application' book, with emphasis on praise.

Inyang Ukot

ACKNOWLEDGMENT

I write to recognize and appreciate the contribution of my wife, Sarah Inyang Ukot, mainly in the form of encouragement to continue with this work to the end. My daughters – Grace, Elor, Sarah Jr., and Joy – are acknowledged for agreeing to be given less than adequate time and attention because of the chunk of time that this book consumed while in the making. My sister, Princess Emana T. Okon has been an inspiration.

I acknowledge the patience exhibited by the illustrator – Oluwatosin Haddy Adetoro.

For seeing the value and impact of this book on prospective users and carving out time from his very busy schedule, for an elder statesman, I express profuse thanks to His Eminence Dr. Sunday Mbang, *CON*, for penning the Foreword of this book.

Finally, I acknowledge the strength that our Lord Jesus Christ gave to me to see through the production of this intricate and multi-focus book in spite of the numerous challenges experienced and eventually overcome.

Inyang Ukot

FOREWORD

Dr. Inyang A. Ukot has introduced us to a new and fascinating way of studying the word of God. The Word of God must be so important to us, children of God, because Jesus Christ, the Son of God, was given the name 'The Word' by St. John when he said:

"In the beginning was the word, and the word was with God, and the word was God ... through him all things were made ... in Him was life and that life was the life of men and women ..." (John 1:1-2).

The Psalmist who made the study of the Word of God his priority says: *"How sweet your word to my taste, (it is), sweeter than honey to my mouth ... I gain understanding from your precepts"* (Psalm 119:103-104).

Dr. Ukot's "Ultimate Praise" provides a new and fascinating method for Biblical Christians to study the Word of God. This way of study is different from many others. Anyone who will be willing to saturate himself/herself with "The Ultimate Praise" will be highly blessed spiritually and physically. For according to the author of the Book of Hebrews *"For the word of God is living and active, sharper than any two-edged sword, it penetrates even the dividing of soul and spirit, joints and marrow; it judges the thoughts and attitudes of the heart."* (Hebrews 4:12). The Psalmist had declared, *"For your word is a lamp to my feet and a light to my path."* (Psalm 11:105). To this end, Jewish parents were instructed to teach their children the word of God, to talk about them *"when you sit at home, and when you walk along the road, when you lie down and when you get up."* They were to tie them as symbols on their hands and bind them on their foreheads. They were to write them on the door frames of their houses and on their gates. (Deuteronomy 6:7-9).

You will recall that Jesus Christ used the Word of God to send Satan packing when He was tempted by him. At the cross, Jesus recited Psalm 22, *"My God, my God, why have you forsaken me."* It was the Word of God that helped Him in that difficult time. The old chorus encourages all and sundry to "read (their) Bible and pray every day if (they) wanted to grow."

Dr. Ukot has provided a rather fascinating and interesting method to achieve this goal for your own benefit. Make reading the Word of God a habit daily and you will never regret it. I, therefore, highly recommend this Praise Book to all who name the Name of Jesus Christ, all the chosen people of God, the messengers of God and all children of God Almighty, to spend some time with Ultimate Praise every day and you will not regret it. Rather, you will thank me for doing so.

My Apostolic Blessings.
His Eminence Dr. Sunday MBANG, *CON.*
Past Prelate, Methodist Church Nigeria
Former President, Christian Association of Nigeria
Former President, World Methodist Council

PREFACE

A cursory look at our world shows that many people have been made to believe, unfortunately wrongly, that the Bible is an irrelevant, ancient book that is fit for the archives. Without any effort at confirming the assertion, many have considered it to be the truth, and so they take the whole thing – hook, line and sinker.

However, a detailed study shows any reader that the Bible is one of the most interesting and relevant literature for our times. It is, perhaps, the reality that five years in many spheres of specialization in the world today is time too long to maintain certain concepts and practices (say, in medicine and ICT) that fuels the extension of the fact to the Bible and its contents. Why not, many would argue, seeing that the Bible is older than them all?

The above aside, we know that we are in a world where people's interests are rapidly shifting, and novelty is frequently accepted before being analyzed for verity of its content. We also know that the one who shouts loudest on various social media is usually heard first, and most. Unfortunately, Scripture does not always work that way, and attempts at projecting matters of the Spirit with similar zest may be counter-productive for some people.

These, and other issues, bring us to Ultimate Praise. Although there are a number of songs in the Bible e.g. Moses' and Miriam's song in Exodus 15:1–21, and Mary's song in Luke 1:46–55, the Book of Psalms has the highest concentration of songs in the entire Bible. It is actually a book of songs. For Ultimate Praise, the psalms were chosen because even though they are basically songs, they contain a lot of information that shows God's dealings with humankind, nations, people-groups, families, and individuals. The principles apply to people of all age-groups, and Ultimate Praise is written for all who can read.

When you are at the airport awaiting your flight to be announced; when you are in the airplane for a long flight (and cannot/should not use your 'phone); when you are at the park, or at home, and you want to get some insight from the Scripture using a rather simple book; when you want to study a subject and you want a summary of that subject before you choose a more detailed mode/material for study, Ultimate Praise is the resource that will not only keep you occupied but also certainly bless you. It should not take you more than a few minutes to go through one or two of the write-ups. From the Table of Contents, you can readily choose and read on a topic that interests or intrigues you.

There are also a few Puzzles of the Word Search type towards the end of the book. You should find them stimulating and engaging.

The author wishes you blessings from the Lord as you choose to use part of your day to occupy your mind and spirit exercising with this book that is based entirely on the Book of Psalms. For full benefits, kindly use this book alongside any form of the New International Version (NIV) of the Bible.

INTRODUCTION

You are invited to Ultimate Praise. The apostle Paul admonished us in 1Thessalonians 5:16–18 to rejoice, pray and give thanks *always and in all circumstances* because this is the will of God in Christ Jesus for us. Praise is a veritable tool for achieving success in living a desirable Christian life to the glory of our God, and to the benefit of the individual, and society. Achieving Ultimate Praise demands focusing on Him, and not on yourself and your favorable or unpleasant circumstances. The writers of the Book of Psalms did not lie on a bed of roses, but had experiences similar to yours and mine; yet they wrote and sang these very instructive songs.

Please read, *and re-read*, the short articles which are really nuggets of wisdom to help you with various aspects of life's up-and-down experiences. At the time of using this book you may not have had some (or any) of the experiences that the psalms address, but there is no harm in still getting a good understanding of them by returning to study the Book of Psalms after you might have finished reading the various topics that Ultimate Praise covers.

By the time you go through this book, you should have a wider and deeper understanding of the issues addressed in the Book of Psalms; they are a good reflection of the contents of the rest of the Bible. Do not forget that the Book of Psalms covers historical, spiritual, messianic, political, social, economic, and contemporary personal matters from which each reader can gain very valuable insights.

The author wishes that this input will encourage you to show more interest in the well-loved, but little-applied, Book of Psalms. Showing interest in, and using the wealth of information from, the psalms is better than staying satisfied with simply memorizing some of them, the way many have been taught to do right from childhood.

Be blessed and have fun.

Inyang Ukot

HOW TO USE

Dear reader, please note that you need a copy of the New International Version (NIV) of the Bible either as hard copy or electronic copy to benefit fully from this book, including the short puzzle section of the book.

The main portion of Ultimate Praise contains write-ups that you can read from the first to the last or you simply select the ones to read according to your interest, present circumstance, spiritual or other needs.

With respect to the puzzle section, the clue words are just extract from the selected Bible passages. To get the link and context of the words you need to read the particular psalm, or you will simply be doing an exercise in finding words.

Each puzzle has the following parts:
The body (web or grid) of letters – within which all the clue words are hidden, and should be found;
Clues – These are words listed in capital letters.

Finding the answers:
The answers are arranged horizontally, vertically and obliquely.
There are eight possible directions that the words can take viz:

- From left to right (horizontally)
- From right to left (horizontally)
- From up to down (vertically)
- From down to up (vertically)
- From up left to down, right (obliquely)
- From down, right to up left (obliquely)

- From up right to down left (obliquely)
- From down left to up right (obliquely)

Have a rewarding time, as you read through the various articles and do the puzzle exercises.

CHAPTER 1

The Key to Blessings from God

Psalm 1:1–6

Living for God is a daily choice like the choice to sit, stand, and walk. Of the three actions, the logical first is to sit and the next is stand, before walk. We know that babies who sit have made some achievement compared with the time they were being carried around by people. This study shows the bad spiritual trend we should avoid i.e. moving from walking, standing, and finally to sitting.

Older children, young people and adults have the choice of who they sit with e.g. to discuss things. What happens when you stand, or walk with people? Who are those in your chosen group and what do you discuss? Let the people you mingle with, plan with and do things with fall into the category that God will be glad to *watch over*, verse 6a, and the decisions you make and actions you take also be the ones that the Lord will surely watch over. God sees all things but He does not watch over all ways – He chooses what He watches over, or endorses.

Many of us want to prosper in what we do – studies at school, relationships, e.g. friendship, marriage, family, etc., business, career; the *key* is "Make choices daily to please God." If you choose to do even the simple things of daily living to honor God, your life will be pleasant and fruitful all-round, like the tree that is planted and grows by the riverside.

What are those things that you should avoid and the ones you should pay attention to? *Walking* in step with the wicked, verse 1, shows that you agree with them; so, avoid that. *Standing* with sinners, verse 1, suggests that they have gripped your attention; so, ensure that it does not happen. *Sitting* in the company of mockers, verse 1, means that you have finally become comfortable doing ridiculous things; avoid it like the plague. It is obvious that it is when 'your delight (interest) is in the law of the Lord and you meditate (dwell on, churn, or ruminate) on God's Law (Word) in the daytime and at night' that you please Him. In summary, the key is avoiding both clear and subtle negative things and choosing what is right in God's sight, even if those right things are not popular.

CHAPTER 2

God Laughs at His Opponents

Psalm 2:1–12

The Bible tells us that wicked leaders or people in authority plot against even God. Why then do we think that they should not plot against us? Human beings are somewhat forgetful and have a general tendency of believing and concluding that what happened to another person will not happen to them. People who have any form of power or authority over other people have convinced themselves that they are immune to disciplinary action as they can easily play the trump card. This is true, otherwise people who have studied history would know that history repeats itself – it may not happen in the same place, but anywhere the same errors or actions are made, the results will be similar. This position of advantage that some people find themselves in actually confuses them, and they feel that they will hold it forever, and even if they don't, there are people that they have placed in important positions to do their bidding.

Unfortunately, these people take this faulty frame of mind to a laughable extent. What they do to people they consider to be beneath them, they extend it to God and plot against God, His plans and His Anointed (The Christ), verse 2. The same God who derides these high-ranking, confident persons in various parts of the earth, goes on to advise them on the right way they should go. If you pay attention to verses 10–12 you will find three important words viz.: wise, serve, and kiss. The first is that they should turn from the unwise belief and act of opposing God, verse 10. The next is that they should become subject to God, and actually serve Him, verse 11. Finally, they should become so close and endeared to God as to *kiss* His Son. This advice that God gave them is the same counsel He still gives to anyone who is yet to be a child of God.

You have read in verse 4 that God laughs and scoffs at His opponents. To be able to laugh at them like God does, we must ensure God is with us in spite of the fact that people may be plotting against our success even when we are right. Before that, are you kissing His Son?

CHAPTER 3

God Answers My Cry

Psalm 3:1–8

A way God blesses and delivers His people is to make wicked people powerless over us. Sadly, people who do not wish us well may be closely related with us. Things may have gone on normally for many months or years between you and another person or group of people; then out of the blues, you get shocked to find that the person or people you trusted and were very free with, just chose not to relate normally with you anymore. When you *cry for deliverance* the way this psalmist did, it does not mean that you are in need of deliverance from a spiritual problem; you could simply need deliverance (or freedom) from such ugly situations. This is the kind of situation that King David, who wrote this psalm, found himself in. You will remember that his son, Absalom, not just plotted against him but was ready to take over the throne forcefully. Sometimes, when you pray to God to deliver you it does not mean that you cannot do anything – you may be in a position to solve that problem, but God usually has a *better way* of doing it.

A person without teeth, or with multiple fractures of the jaw bone, cannot bite. From afar, and when you are in trouble, you may not realize that those who are against your welfare have problems too. Some children of God prefer God *killing* such people – and they pray prayers in that line. Is that the kind of request you think you should make to God? If you do like King David, you will find that God will fight and do an excellent job of it for you.

CHAPTER 4

God Allows Man Authority Over His Creation

Psalm 8:1–9

This is another psalm by David. He considered the heavens and the entire earth, and told God who created them that He is really majestic as the work of His hands proved His majesty and glory. He then decided to look at humankind and placed humanity side-by-side the sun, moon, stars, (and, as we know today, the entire universe) and he saw human beings as less than a speck of the entire creation. Should we do this same exercise, we will also feel humbled that God even shows interest in us – verse 4. More astonishing is that fact that God put everything He created under humankind's feet, thus giving us authority over all – verse 6. The exception seems to be fellow human beings. It shows a very high level of trust in a person for you to allow them control over what rightly belongs to you. It is especially true, when you allow them control over everything you have. Your mind should go quickly to Potiphar and Joseph. Potiphar had an exception too; it was his wife. God must have had (and still has) a strong belief in the potentials that He built into us to oversee the affairs of His creation.

But people prefer to lord it over other people. How do you think our world – and indeed God's entire creation – would be if humankind spent time and energy to exercise authority over God's creation instead of oppressing, suppressing and terrorizing fellow humans? As a child, do you think bullying at school or in the neighborhood is what God expects you to do? Would He tell you *well done* for bullying other children? As an employer, supervisor, manager, lecturer, manufacturer, judge, physician, etc. do you think that the knowledge and authority that God has given you are for you to make other people's lives miserable? If you do, you are mistaken. Also, the air, land and bodies of water that God has given us are for us to manage properly. This simply means that we must not continue to pollute the air, poison our surface and underground waters and the sea creatures, or destroy our forests and carry out activities that denude our land, etc., but protect them for now and for the benefit of future generations.

CHAPTER 5

God's Kind of Judgment

Psalm 9:1–10

Judgment is a word that some people like and others loathe; the former are those who expect and receive positive judgment, but the latter are people who know that they are in the wrong and do not expect anything other than judgment of condemnation. God is really a righteous Judge and when we decide to do a detailed personal study, we will always conclude that holiness and righteousness are what God does not joke with. He even told us in Matthew 6:33 that righteousness is what we should seek or pursue primarily, if we want other things pertaining to life to be added to us. But how is God's judgment like?

God's kind of judgment is based on truth, uprightness, fairness and what is right. In a normal human court what the judge does is to try to sift the truth from lies – and, sometimes, that may be an arduous, if not impossible, task. But not so with God – as He knows the *truth* already. His judgment is also based on *uprightness* and not subject to crookedness predicated on bribery and corruption. His judgment is *fair,* as God is not a respecter of persons – rich or poor, old or young; His judgment is always *right,* and so is not subject to review. This is why whatever God's Word says is wrong, is unchangeably wrong – and we should not try to give it any other coloration. His right stays so. God's judgment does not have *no go areas* – He judges all who inhabit the earth, verse 8. Only God can judge the way He does, and when He does it, it is crystal clear that it is His handiwork, verse 16. Children, adults, kings and the poor can, and will, be judged by God.

We can throw up our hands in surrender, and say that only God can judge the way it is described in this chapter. It is true, but does that mean we should not attempt to copy our Heavenly Father? Don't very young children watch and copy what parents and other adults do? In the various judgments we pass at home, etc. we would not be wrong to start basing them on *truth, uprightness (straightness), fairness,* and *the right*. When judged by God, will you get *well done* from Him?

CHAPTER 6

Thoughts and Deeds of Wicked People

Psalm 10:1–15

One of the characteristics of the wicked is that they do not have God in their thoughts and deeds. Verse 4 summarizes it by stating that wicked people are so full of themselves that there is no space left for them to think of God – and, therefore, no way for them to have anything to do with Him. The same verse indicates that they do not seek God. If they do not seek the Person, how will they follow or obey Him?

Their thoughts: Their thoughts consist of the following: They think that they are secure, verse 6; they think that God does not see or notice, verse 11; they conclude that God will never hold them to account, verse 13; they also believe that God is like men who do not have the capacity to find out everything, verse 15. They are neither moved nor feel concerned, when they inflict pain and damage on people.

Their actions: They do things that cause pain and grief to other people, verse 2. They encourage evil by congratulating greedy people, verse 3. Their evil actions bring prosperity to them, verse 5. They reject God's law, verse 5. They tell lies and threaten people, verse 7. They murder people, verses 8—10. They do not live for God, though they may pretend to love God. The wicked also borrow and do not repay, or return what they borrowed, Psalm 37:21.

Very early, children must be taught to embrace God and godly values; otherwise, Satan will plant wickedness in their hearts and make them think that wickedness is normal. The adults in the lives of children must make provision for time to instruct them in godly ways, apart from living the Christian life for the young ones to admire and emulate; otherwise, the danger is children's exposure to the lie that God will not notice, verse 11 or that the wicked are secure, verse 6, or admire their arrogance from the prosperity that may follow their wickedness verses 2–5. God will hold people to account – verses 13 and 15.

CHAPTER 7

Good Foundation, No Shaking

Psalm 15:1–5

A good foundation ensures that a house does not shake; even in earthquake-prone parts of the world, a building on a foundation designed to withstand earthquake may shake but will not fall. Our lives should be built on good/solid foundation. This assumes right timing – which, in this case, has childhood as the best *construction period*. This psalm lists the following as the *materials* for this good foundation: 'doing the right things', verse 2; speaking the truth, verse 2; good use of the tongue, verse 3; refusing to honor vile persons, verse 4; honoring godly people and godliness, verse 4; keeping promises, verse 4; not putting additional financial burden on the poor, verse 5; and avoiding bribery, verse 5. We shall dwell a little on bribery in the next paragraph.

Bribe. Bribery. These words are with human beings. Depending on the society, it could be full of giving and taking of bribe or it could be minimal – but it is there. Bribery causes a lot havoc everywhere it is found. It, generally, does not allow things to work well. Right is treated as wrong, wrong is enhanced to the place of prominence and acceptability, and the dirty is laundered or cleaned up with proceeds of the bribery. Bribery does not allow people to have interest in excellence, does not encourage productivity and stifles talent. Many who engage in bribery consider two people or two parties only; unfortunately, there is usually a third person or third party in every case of bribery. The Bible calls this third person or party *the innocent*, verse 5, and bribery is a crime or offence against them, apart from God. This person bears the brunt of bribery; e.g. bribery to enable a prospective student or employee gain admission into the university (college) or gain employment sees to it that the qualified *innocent's* place is taken and given to another person who is less deserving. Apart from God, think of the third person you are about to offend any time you face the temptation to be involved in bribery. If you stay away from bribery, you will live within your means and God will bless you and your legitimate income. You will also be a more disciplined person.

CHAPTER 8

Praise Be to God, My Adviser

Psalm 16:1–11

Counsel is very important in everyone's life. Interestingly, this importance is a two-edged sword in the sense that counsel can be uplifting or destructive. It is essential to be sure of at least two things: the quality of counsel and source of counsel. Before we go further, it must be mentioned that counsel may be from a person or a thing. The person may be a parent, spouse, friend, sibling, teacher, foreman, manager, employer, etc. The thing may be a book, movie, meeting, sermon, etc.

From the above introduction, who or what do you take instructions or advice from? The ultimate source of counsel is God. It is like purchasing an item and finding the manufacturer-provided user manual. You may choose to refer to it, or may ignore it and rather use the equipment the way you want. God is our Manufacturer. It pays to make our hearts *hear* from God. It is only when we clearly hear from God that we can safely follow our hearts, verse 7 – otherwise, our hearts may misguide us.

In the actual or figurative "night times or seasons" (verse 7, KJV) of our lives, we must hear God clearly or we can drift and take counsel or advice from anywhere and anybody. These are times when the happenings in our lives are unclear, confusing and frightening to us – and we just don't get it. If you make God your focus every time, you will stand firm and will not be moved by problems of life – verse 8. You may be in such a situation right now and may be fully assured that if you dwell on this psalm and similar ones, you will find your feet and bearing.

The above does not mean that you should not listen to what people may tell you. Proverbs 11:14 clearly tells us that there is safety in the multitude of counsel. People give counsel, sometimes unsolicited. Counselors must be professionally equipped. The important thing is for you to match human counsel with the 'spiritual compass' that does not fail – that compass is God's Word.

CHAPTER 9

The Lord Sustains Me

Psalm 18:25–36

In verse 35 we read that God's right hand sustained the psalmist and the purpose was to make him great. Sustenance is a means of support or maintenance for a person or thing. The first few verses of this psalm show sustenance or support, viz.: Strength – Every child depends on the strength of parents for support e.g. carrying the baby or later helping the child make first walking attempts to avoid falls, verse 1; Rock, fortress and shield – the conies or hyrax know that without the crags in a *rock* they are very vulnerable; kings and top government officials of old knew that *fortresses* gave them protection; soldiers knew that *shields* protected them during wars, verse 2.

In the latter part of the psalm (the emphasis of this write-up) the psalmist created the picture of the deer (hind, hart) that is still able to live, move and run on difficult mountain terrain with assured support – verse 33; he also said in verse 36 that God provided adequate space for his feet ensuring that he did not buckle at the ankles.

In everybody's life there shall be times when we desperately need support; it does not matter how many years we have walked with the Lord, our age, educational, intellectual, financial or social status. We must be wise and focused enough to ask for deliverance at such times.

Indeed, God gives us strength and provides us with deliverance. If we are weak and give up, when God's deliverance comes, we may not see it and may not key into it – verses 17–19, 32–37. It is unfortunate that many people (perhaps, including you and me) do not realize that whatever greatness we have achieved was/is the result of sustenance by God. We must show gratitude to God who has prevented us from slipping in all ways.

CHAPTER 10

Glory in God's Word and Creation

Psalm 19:1–14

God's glory is found in creation and His Word, the Bible. There is so much grandeur in both instruments, for the Bible does not contest with any other book, philosophy or intellectual to confirm its relevance or veracity – the truth is there and people will either get it or miss it. Ditto with God's creation – the psalmist started this psalm by referring to the heavenly bodies, the ones we see being the skies, stars, sun and moon. We know that there are many more, and that space is endless, virtually doing 'its thing,' not minding us.

As earlier stated, the Bible and creation do not have to shout to get our attention for they continuously – day and night – tell us of God's wisdom, verses 1–3. In verse 4, King David told us that the voice and unspoken *words* of God's creation get to every nook and cranny of the earth.

We are familiar with the fact that a bridegroom or champion does not extol or clap for themselves. In certain cultures, elderly people who have never stood up for their young ones, gladly do so on the wedding day, when the bride and groom march into the church or into the reception hall after the church wedding. This is an honor. People hail, clap and get excited for a champion but the champion that does so for self will be considered funny and vain.

Yes, there is glory in God's creation and His Word. God uses His Word to warn us and guide us into (or to remain in) His glory and when we heed God's warning, we benefit by receiving a great reward – verse 11. Let our prayer be that the words of our mouths, and the meditation of our hearts, should be acceptable in God's sight – our Strength and Redeemer – see verse 14.

CHAPTER 11

The Day He Was Crucified

Psalm 22:1–18 *KJV*

To get the full picture of what happened on the day that Jesus was crucified, you should read and ponder on the entire chapter and not stop with the eighteen verses used for this chapter. That day was a unique day in the history of humankind and confirmed long-standing prophecy about our Lord's suffering, crucifixion, and slow but painful death – for no sin of His.

Satan unleashed the most severe affliction and pain on our Lord the day He was crucified. For the first time the Christ experienced a gap, distance or separation from His Father – verses 1, 2, 11, 19.

Christ was "worm, not man", verse 6; "reproached", verse 6; "despised", verse 6; "laughed to scorn", verse 7; "gaped upon", verse 13; "poured out like water", verse 14; and taunted by "shooting out of the lip and shaking of the head" by both soldiers and onlookers, verse 7. His bones were "out of joint", verse 14; heart "like wax", verse 14; strength "dried up", verse 15 and tongue "cleaved to his jaw", verse 15.

We thank God that 'posterity' or a 'seed' will serve the Lord Jesus Christ and our generation and future generations, just like past generations, will be told about the wonderful sacrifice which He made on the cross for humankind – verse 30. The sacrificial and gracious events of the day Jesus was crucified paved the way to His resurrection, ascension and living on making intercession for us, thus making you and me have the chance to key into God's Salvation plan through the said Christ's vicarious suffering, death and eventual resurrection.

CHAPTER 12

The Lord, My Guide

Psalm 23:1–6

Presence is what people want in relationships. Presence is not only physical presence, as it is possible to be available at a place, meeting, function and not be fully involved in the goings-on there. We all must have experienced talking with someone only to find that we were virtually talking to ourselves, as the person was either not paying attention to us and our talk or was actually doing something else that they considered more important. Teachers do not like it.

This is probably the best known and most easily recited psalm; in this extraordinary psalm, King David tells us the benefits of God's presence and guidance. All – boys, girls, young persons, men and women – want the Lord's goodness and mercy to follow them throughout their lives. There is, however, a condition that you and I must accept and meet: to allow God to guide or lead us in right or righteous paths, daily. It is easy to want goodness and mercy but not so easy to let God lead us and be the controller of our lives.

There are so many who are competing to lead us – friends, school mates, family members, colleagues at work, philosophies, whatever is in vogue, etc.; these may sometimes lead us aright but at other times, they can lead us the wrong way. Only God can lead/guide us consistently in the right/ righteous way *if we allow Him*.

Our prayer is that our real and deep-seated desire shall be to submit our thoughts, plans and actions into God's hands, remembering that sheep have the tendency to go astray (see Luke 15:3–7), even when the shepherd is available and willing to guide. The contents of Psalm 23 will materialize in our lives only if we really want them to.

CHAPTER 13

Glory to The Maker and Owner of All

Psalm 24:1–10

Kings, queens, presidents, governors and people that are like them do not go to every occasion. When they appear, the gathering changes and the venue is frequently given special attention in terms of decoration, security arrangements, etc. This caliber of persons become objects of attraction and interest and the program for the events they attend must make provision for them to feature. This glory, splendor or grandeur associated with them is in spite of the fact that they are humans – but let the truth be told, they are different. Not everyone can or will be like them.

God is the Maker and Owner of all things. He is glorious and to Him belongs ultimate glory. Above is a brief description of human glory, but whatever is ascribed to human royalty is ephemeral and changes hands. God's glory does not change hands. From time-to-time, God may make certain people taste His glory and we know that Jesus mentioned in John 17:22 that He has given to all Christians His glory. But how much do we appreciate and how well do we apply the glory? It is glorious to go up the mountain of the Lord and stand in His holy place, see verse 3. God's glory is associated with blessings to His people; these blessings come with the gift of right standing and practice of right living (righteousness), verse 4.

If we all desired this kind of blessings, we would not trouble ourselves and other people so much by causing pain, sorrow, anger and hatred in pursuit of only *material blessings and prosperity* that we cannot take away when we eventually leave this earth. Jesus told us to seek the kingdom of God and His righteousness, and all the things that people toil or scramble for will be added to us by God, Matthew 6: 33.

CHAPTER 14

Protected When There Is Trouble

Psalm 27:1–10

In those times when we are faced with difficulties, problems or challenges, God expects us not to fear but to know that He will protect us. Many Christians believe their lives should be rosy and jolly, day-in-day-out and year-in-year-out, but Scripture does not support that belief.

It is usually interesting and encouraging to listen to, or read about, people's testimonies regarding what the Lord did for them. Have you considered that the experiences that led to the testimonies, most likely, were not interesting in many cases? Agreed, it may have been interesting if God touched someone to grant you a particularly big favor that you may not even have asked for.

Scripture tells us that it is *"when"* and not *"if"* the enemy advances against us ....that the enemy will stumble and fall; it is *"when"* and not *"if"* we pass through the waters and fire that the Lord will be with us and protect us – Isaiah 43:2. Nobody gets excited when the government sends an army to besiege one in one's home. But something close to that could happen to a person and their family members. It is when God provides protection and safety in such undesirable conditions that our heads will be lifted high above the heads of those who surround us with wishes, plots and actual acts of evil – verses 5 and 6.

Let us face life fearlessly. Even if we fear we can lose the fear as we allow God to work on us through experiences that make us fear less and less until we become fearless. For our lives to have God as our Stronghold and be filled with God's light and salvation, we must deliberately live lives of seeking God from the depth of our hearts – verses 1 and 8.

CHAPTER 15

The Voice of The Lord

Psalm 29:1–9

Successful and long-lasting relationships owe those qualities partly, and importantly, to 'voice.' This is because in the majority of cases we need to hear and understand each other clearly to relate properly. Babies learn very early to identify the voices and faces of the people closest to them, especially their parents. They do not talk but they certainly build into their memories that ability to know with certainty who is who. They therefore differentiate very easily who the parents are and who strangers are. In our relationships with ourselves in adulthood we do not drop what we did in childhood but actually build on it.

When we say we relate with God, it is also essential for us to know when God is saying something and what He is saying to us. The voice of the Lord is what we read of in this psalm and are trying to study and understand the basics. This psalm shows us the opposite of the voice of the Lord we know as "the still small voice" – 1 Kings 19: 12. Here the voice of the Lord is powerful and majestic, and manifests in various parts of the earth e.g. forests, thunder, fire, wilderness or desert, seas and oceans and floods. Though we know that wildfires, sandstorms, hurricanes, earthquakes, tsunamis, etc. wreak monumental havoc, they are actually demonstrations of the *voice of the Lord*. God speaks through nature and from the voice, we are forced to hear and understand His greatness and our vulnerability. If God were to throw His weight around, how comfortable would we be? God actually keeps the elements in check most of the time – and it is for the general good of humankind. As we listen, we shall hear God speak to us either softly or loudly. We just have to do the needful.

CHAPTER 16

Confess and Be Forgiven

Psalm 32:1–7

In life, we have all been faced with the situation where we want to put the cart before the horse; or even to do away with the horse, without being interested in doing the horse's work ourselves. This is especially so in spiritual matters, where we do not see any physical person insisting that the right things be done. Don't you remember when as a young child you felt you should eat without being disturbed by mummy calling you to give a helping hand in the kitchen? But food preparation naturally happens before food consumption. In spiritual matters, both children and adults not only entertain similar wishful thinking but actually try to put it into practice. It is because of this, that people tend to push sin into the background, or give it mild and fanciful name tags like 'faults', 'errors', 'slip of tongue', 'I did not mean it', 'flesh and blood', 'holier-than-thou', etc., when matters of sin ought to be (or, are) addressed.

Because sin is really a shameful thing, people of all age brackets want to hide sin. At other times people block their hearts, and make sin look popular or glamorous – they then commit such sins openly and unabashedly. No matter the type of sin, people tend to hide sin from God. This does not work and does not pay.

Hiding sin is a form of self-punishment – verses 3 and 4. You will notice the word 'cover' in two places (verses 1 and 5), and by two persons – (God, in verse 1) and (a human being, in verse 5). It is better to acknowledge (accept, own up to) sin, then confess it to God and, in godly sorrow, ask God for forgiveness. It is the forgiveness we get from God that covers our sin. This train of actions brings Salvation which enables a person to face God as a son or daughter; and also face Satan as his victor, and no longer as a victim. God covering our sins is, therefore, effective. When we, as humans, make attempts at covering sin it is worthless, as we only succeed in deceiving ourselves, and not God. Whatever action we eventually take is our choice.

CHAPTER 17

The Lord Deserves My Praise

Psalm 33:1–9

The psalmist starts this psalm by telling us how to praise this great God who deserves our praise. You will observe that he says we should play the instruments skillfully, and shout for joy during the praise. What we notice in many Christian gatherings is much shouting during preaching of sermons, and when giving testimonies, etc. We believe that there is a difference. When people of God sing praises to Him there is no sound amplification and so they can **shout with their normal voices**; when there is already sound amplification for the speaker or choir, additional screaming could make the hearers miss the contents of the message or song.

The Lord deserves our praise and we should praise Him with both our voices and man-made instruments of praise. This Psalm mentions just a few of the reasons we should praise God e.g. His word is right; His works are based on truth; He loves righteousness and justice; His goodness is seen in the things He created and put on, or in, the earth; the whole universe was made by Him, verses 2–6. We rejoice that we have summer and winter, dry and rainy seasons, only at the right times.

This psalm tells us the appropriate people to give God praise that He deserves; it calls them *the upright* in verse 1. Might it be that God does not want praise from just anyone? Do you think that your country's president would be very pleased if a band of well-known criminals were the only ones praising him or her?

As children and adults, we should praise this just and loving God who does not fail, using our mouths and any musical instrument we can operate skillfully – but make sure that we are in tune with Him. Yes, God is faithful and deserves our praise.

CHAPTER 18

How to Get My Heart's Desires from God

Psalm 37:1–11

God, like our earthly parents, has shown us what to do to get our requests from Him. Many children and adults believe that God owes them the debt of taking care of, and providing for, them. God has put in the earth and our environment all we need to live on. When we want our deepest desires to be met by this loving God, we have a part to play – that part is found in verses 3–5 i.e. to trust and depend on God, commit our ways and lives to God, and take delight or pleasure in the Lord and what pleases Him. Are we ready to meet the conditions for this worthwhile relationship?

The three ingredients of our role shall be briefly explained here: a) *Trusting and depending on God* – Even among humans, trust is important to achieve positive things. If you go to the provisions section of a supermarket or shopping mall, pay and pick up canned food, you trust that it is the canned food you expect; if it turns out to be something else, or food of lower quality, will you be willing to continue patronizing that manufacturer? b) *Committing our ways and lives to God* – To receive the services of a cab company and its driver, you must commit your safety into the driver believing in their experience and professionalism, apart from proper maintenance of the cab. It is because some people do not trust God fully that they handle some aspects of their lives contrary to what is clearly stated in God's Word. c) *Taking delight in what pleases God* – A child who loves the father and mother will delight in doing what pleases the parents, even if personal inconvenience results from it. The same thing happens if we really love Jesus Christ.

To get the desires of our hearts (verses 6 and 11) from God, we need to pay attention to these three guidelines and put them into practice. It is when we put into practice what we say we believe, that we will find that what we believe has a solid foundation, God. Getting the desires of our hearts is synonymous with getting reasons for testimonies.

CHAPTER 19

Our Lifetime on Earth Is Short

Psalm 39:4–13

It needs no great elaboration for you and I to agree that most of us crave for similar things. This is true when you consider the part of the world where you are in, and sometimes the small community where you were born or reside in. This could mean that at a certain age you want to go to school or learn a trade; later, you may desire to travel out of your local community and live in a large city; at a particular time, you may want to make and own a certain amount of money and acquire certain possessions; surely most youths choose a career and grow in it; young adults want to get married and start raising children, etc.

How do you assess yourself: Very beautiful, strong, intelligent, rich, powerful, influential or very poor, weak, uncreative, etc.? But how does God assess *us all*? God sees us more deeply than we can imagine. Verses 4–6 show that God sees us as frail, busy but vain, and the length of our days (our age) as nothing. Let us see ourselves the way God sees us and we shall learn, know and pay attention to what are important – and this does not mean encouraging laziness or lack of ambition. It simply means putting everything we plan, desire and achieve in the right perspective.

If you divide Eternity (Infinity) by our length of days (120 years for the oldest of persons), the answer lets you know *why* God says our age is as nothing to Him. We must ensure good relations with God through Jesus Christ, His Son. Because every time we wake up and embrace a new day, and every time we celebrate a New Year, our lives get shorter by one day and year respectively, we must live the unknown balance satisfactorily. Let us live our lives to ensure that our years count before God and not just to count our years on earth.

CHAPTER 20

A Strong Desire for God

Psalm 42:1–5

This psalm tells us about a person longing for God the way a deer longs for water. In the case of a deer, severe thirst makes it show its desire for water by panting; if it is human thirst, we do not search for streams for the water is very likely somewhere in our homes, e.g. the refrigerator. Because potable water is readily available in the homes of readers of this book, they may not understand people in remote communities that are in lack of water in certain countries of the world. They will also not readily understand the symbol of thirst for water, as thirst for God.

This particular psalmist shows us a strong desire for God, in spite of being in very difficult situations. If you have ever been in a situation where people begin to ask you face-to-face *Where is your God?* you will understand that such conditions spell despondency, and not a greater desire for God. But would you succumb to sadness, dejection or frustration?

Being with the crowd in church (verse 4b) to attend services and praise God is good. The crowd, however, does not take away the deep desires and aches of our hearts. You and I need to have that spiritual buffer or 'shock absorber' to confront these realities when we are alone.

Everybody (boy, girl, man or woman) will face serious problems in life from time to time. These challenges are of different types – academic decline, work-related upheavals, family disruptions, business downturn, etc. Having a deep-seated desire for God is an attribute or state of mind and spirit that will enable us successfully weather these storms of life, verse 8.

Let your desire for God be like the desire a thirsty deer has for scarce water.

CHAPTER 21

What Do You Delight In?

Psalm 43:1–5

There are no two of us that are exact in every way, and that is one of the reasons that one of the psalms records that we are fearfully and wonderfully made; there is therefore no duplicate of you – God made you to be special or unique. When you know of a certainty that you do not have a duplicate key to your place of residence, documents safe or car, the natural thing to do is to take more care in handling that key, the entire purpose being to ensure its safety. You will not delight in doing things that could easily make you lose that key.

As mentioned above, you are completely different from any other person, alive or dead. There are many similarities though, but these are group similarities. What I call group similarities could be height, weight, complexion, language, residential area, choice of hairstyle or dressing, and other likes, taboos, etc. If you live in a residential estate, there could be pre-set rules regarding ways of doing things and so you will be similar to other residents in the way and times of refuse disposal, etc.; in the same way, there may be a dress code for employees in a factory or ladies in a wedding train, making them look similar.

It is, therefore, clear that there could be group delights though the emphasis of this write-up is individual delight. What are the things that you delight in? What would the answer be if there was no other person for reference; that is, nobody to criticize or give you a pat on the back for demonstrating your delights? That is what we are referring to.

Surely, since God is the only one who knows our hearts and, consequently, what we really delight in, would it not be important for us to care about what we delight in, though they could be hidden to people? This psalmist said in verse 4 that he would go to God's altar – *indeed to God, who he called his 'joy and delight.'* Did you know that you should place God at the very top of your list of delights?

CHAPTER 22

Knowing Your Family History

Psalm 44: 1–3

Family history is one of the things that many people take pride in. To be able to take pride in historical matters, any group of people have to know their history. This group of people can be families, as the title of this write-up indicates; the people could be an entire nation, or a race. Knowledge of the history has a lot to do with the veracity of the contents of the history, whether documented in one form of writing or another – or verbally transmitted. Whatever form the history takes, the most important element or factor seems to be truthfulness of the original witnesses and/ or writers.

It is natural for people to make known the positive aspects of their history, and to minimize the negative parts. In very simple terms, it is easier and more comfortable to mention the things considered to be success and simply forget or disregard the failures. It, however, appears that it is good to learn from both. It is when a people know the mistakes of their forebears that they will not repeat them – unless they do not care. It is also when they know what were responsible for the success stories of their ancestors that they will walk in their steps.

Psalm 44 in its first three verses summarizes the history of Israel. You will remember that they started off as just a family. What is instructive in these verses is that the psalmist ascribes their history to God's help and grace. If you begin by knowing that what you achieve in life is by God's grace and help, you will be able to tell your children so – and your family history will eventually reflect it. Our failures can benefit from His deliverance.

CHAPTER 23

In What or Whom Do You Boast?

Psalm 44: 4–8

In this short passage we find three weapons, two of which can be classified as ancient and one as ancient-and-modern. The ancient weapons are sword and bow; the ancient-and-modern weapon is God. We shall briefly consider the usefulness of these weapons.

Sword: A sword is a piercing and, possibly, penetrating instrument of war. It is hand-held and should not be dropped, otherwise the owner or the soldier to whom it is assigned becomes very vulnerable. A sword serves as an offensive and defensive weapon. The summary is that a sword is designed for battles in which the enemy is very close and within your arms' reach.

Bow: A bow is a weapon crafted from wooden or other material that will not break when bent; it is to the free ends of the bent material that a string is tied tautly. A bow is used alongside arrows, which are stored and carried in a quiver. The bow is used to shoot arrows, one at a time, as required. The direction of aim is dependent on where the enemy is sighted. Good vision, alertness, persistence and strength are valuable when bow and arrows are employed in a battle situation. When used in sports there is obviously room for relaxation. Finally bow and arrows are used for distant objects or enemies – but within range of vision.

God: God is our Ultimate Weapon. He is omniscient and so He knows what and who our enemies are – even when you and I do not know. Whether the enemy is within your reach or very far away, you can use God to overcome. This psalm writer was a very wise man for he said that he refused to boast in his dexterity, experience, sword or bow but in God, verse 8. We can rejoice in having God as the Weapon we can depend on; the other weapons mentioned in this write-up, and other weapons that humanity has used, are all prone to failure – and consequently to disappoint their users. Why boast on what could disappoint at the worst of times?

CHAPTER 24

Wanted: Excellent Kings, Inside and Out

Psalm 45: 1–8

Though this psalm refers to Jesus Christ, the King of Kings, it applies to the writer, King David, and can apply – at a lower level – to our modern leaders. By leaders we mean anybody who holds leadership positions; to make the context more inclusive, e.g. leadership in our families, etc. Excellence is not optimal when only internal or external; for greatest impact, excellence must be inside and out. Other people must benefit from excellence.

The excellence within is referred to as: Grace, verse 2; splendor and majesty, verse 3; truth, humility and justice, verse 4; righteousness, verse 7. When you consider each of these excellent qualities within a person, you find that they enable the person to make decisions and take actions based on them. You cannot uphold truth deep inside you and then practice deception in your business, at school and during interaction with your family members, friends, etc. A just person will demonstrate this virtue of fairness even when not a professional judge.

Excellence on the outside is shown as: Awesome deeds, verse 4; joy, verse 7; fragrance, adornment and music, verse 8. *Awesome deeds* are exactly what you are thinking about – awe-inspiring actions; they cannot be hidden and will always be noticed. You should agree that *joy* is actually in our hearts, but is not satisfied to stay there – joy will almost certainly express itself by coming out to be felt by others; *fragrance* is for the sense of smell; *adornment* is for sight, and music is primarily to satisfy our *hearing*. May your excellence affect you and others who associate with you.

CHAPTER 25

Being the King's Bride

Psalm 45: 9–17

Although this psalm refers to Jesus Christ as the King and His Church (Christians), it can apply to other situations and persons to some extent. People who are born into high status must live honorably. Daughters of kings are held in very high regard and they are especially honored when they are engaged to be married into royalty. There is nothing cheap about king's daughters as they are decked in expensive dressing, including gold – verses 9, 13 and 14. This is what happens on the outside, and people look at this and have admiration for them. In the same way God expects everyone who has a relationship with Him through Jesus Christ, i.e. Christians, to represent Him well by noble acts, outward appearance and in all ways demonstrating honor. We are truly Christ's royal bride, verse 9, and should not make caricature of that status. Our God does not like such misrepresentation or distortion.

Two interesting things are mentioned in this passage as a guide to this beautiful bride. The first one requires that she should pay careful attention. This instruction is about her past, because of the new status. Even though she is a daughter and princess, verses 10 and 14, she must pay attention to the fact that she is *now* a royal bride, verse 9. Whatever high (or even low) status we had we must forget about them, place them in the background of our lives and rather pay close attention to our Lord Jesus. The second thing is that we must honor Jesus Christ with our lives because He is our Lord, verse 11. Isn't it interesting that people of high background are very welcome to Jesus? If they do not come to Jesus, they are the ones that keep themselves back – not Jesus.

CHAPTER 26

God, My Emmanuel

Psalm 46:1–11

Twice, in verses 7 and 11 we read *"The Lord Almighty is with us; the God of Jacob is our fortress."* We already know that the word "Immanuel" or Emmanuel means "God with us." The title 'God, My Emmanuel' therefore means that God is with me. The thought and fact that God is with you and me are very re-assuring, especially when things do not seem to be working for us the way we want. Acknowledging and living in the realization of the presence of God give strength and remove fear. In the popular movie Sound of Music, the children of Captain von Trapp ran to Maria during a thunderstorm. The flashes of lightning were not that threatening, as long as they were with the loving Maria.

We shall do well to consider another aspect of God's presence. This is the aspect that God is all-present (omnipresent) and it is linked with His omniscience, all-knowing characteristic. You may have confidence and strength as stated above when you are in dire straits, but would you feel that comfortable if you gave thought to the fact that the same God is with you whether you are doing what is right or doing what is wrong? It is unnerving, but a constant reminder of this truth will help us choose to, and actually do, what God expects of us to do with regards to our official work, the kind of things we engage in to make money, have children, make progress in career and business, etc. Being in His Presence does a lot for us, and will enable us opt for the straight and narrow path and not follow the multitude.

CHAPTER 27

The God of Costly Redemption

Psalm 49:1–13

The entire Psalm 49 makes very interesting reading for those of us living today – in short, its truth is timeless. However, this write-up concentrates on just a few verses that address the subject of the title.

Redemption which leads to (or is an aspect of) salvation is very costly. We read in verses 1 and 2 that this truth is for everyone – high and low, rich and poor. Nobody can redeem the life of another person, and certainly nobody can give to God the equivalent of the cost of redeeming even one person, verse 7. The psalmist goes on to state, in verse 8, that the reason is that redemption is costly and no payment can suffice.

It is this redemption that is offered to us free. Redemption is costly because the Son of God <u>had to die</u> as payment (redemption price) for our sinfulness. The salvation that Christ offers boys, girls, men and women all over the world is actually free, because there is nothing for us to do than just to accept and receive it. For many people, this is too simple to be true. It is this simplicity that people use to create problems for themselves – and therefore they not only despise redemption but also reject it.

Verse 13 gives the insinuation that people who refuse to trust God and accept His offer of redemption in Jesus Christ are those who trust in themselves. This psalm simply describes them as people that forget that nobody endures, verse 12. Do not be like a drowning person who distrusts and refuses a helping hand because they also think that that act is too simple and easy to save them; rather, trust in Jesus Christ and you will be pleasantly surprised that salvation will be yours.

CHAPTER 28

God's Silence Is Not Consent

Psalm 50:7–21

Many people still believe that God gets impressed by the works of their hands which people see. Even in the days of King Saul, God had said that to obey Him is better than to offer sacrifices to Him, and to pay attention to His Word preferred to offering the fat of rams.

One major difference between God and humankind in the way of doing things is that He prefers us to do things using our volition, simply because he put in us freewill and expects us to use it sensibly. In human systems, we do not believe in waiting for people to use their discretion, and that is precisely why many communities, states and countries have crafted and passed laws that cover very many areas of our lives; it is to the extent that an average citizen who is not a practicing lawyer may not know that some laws are in existence until there is an infraction by them. Sadly, ignorance of the law is not usually accepted as an excuse. Advanced countries have parole officers who keep an eye on assigned offenders who have been placed on parole – this is because the state does not fully trust them to abide by the conditions, or terms, of their parole. God does not do that – rather, He watches silently, and without disrupting our activities.

God is not interested in people who hate to take instructions from Him and do not give heed to His words, verse 17. You should not treat God like a beggar that you despise – and yet you offer Him praise and sacrifices, like He is ignorant rather than all-knowing. He says He is not hungry, verse 12.

He asks in verse 21 when people do the contemptible things earlier listed, do such people really think that He is just like them, simply because He is silent? The answer is, obviously, in the negative. However, He will give His salvation to anybody that is willing to live their life the right way in His sight, verse 23.

CHAPTER 29

A Heart of Repentance

Psalm 51:1–12

What do you do when you commit a sinful act? What do you do when you entertain and nourish sinful thoughts? What some people do is to hide and behave like nothing happened. Other people shrug it off and console themselves with the obvious fact that there are people who do worse things and yet live their lives and do not lose sleep. Yet other people are angry with themselves that they have spoilt their personal or family record; for important or highly-placed people, their disgust is in the fact that the sin could be found out, if not already in the open. There are still other people who seek help, e.g. from pastors, close friends, etc.

What God wants us to do is to have godly sorrow that leads to repentance. Godly sorrow is different from the feeling of embarrassment – which is actually a product of self-pride. Godly sorrow is an awareness of the ugliness of the matter in the eyes of God, even when it is acceptable by the society in which you live. By now it should be clear to the reader that God's standards and societal standards are sometimes not in agreement, and could actually be at loggerheads. The important thing is to determine in your mind what is superior – God's documented opinion that does not change, or public opinion. The answer should be obvious to anyone who thinks both spiritually and rationally.

This inward feeling called repentance comes from conviction which the Spirit of God brings to our realization; repentance is a change of mind and actions and it leads to outward confession to God. True confession is serious heartfelt business with God, and not a yo-yo exercise. Of course, we know that many people would want God to understand, and just forgive people without need for repentance. It does not work so.

Salvation is a free gift but God *rewards* repentance with forgiveness. You certainly know that forgiveness is one of the blessings obtained in salvation.

CHAPTER 30

People That God Despises

Psalm 52: 1–5

It is important for us all to know what we use as our yardstick for assessing people and things. It is because we tend to make mistakes of judgment that we sometimes compare goats with cows or lions with cats. It is true that goats and cows eat grass, and that lions and cats eat flesh but the similarity ends there. Apart from making comparisons, the other very important thing that we do is to make choices or take a stand. It is not strange to say that we are in an age when there is a lot of advertisement. Advertisement provides us with information that is occasionally unsolicited and may sometimes be irritating, if not offensive. It is because advertisement is almost ubiquitous that we find ourselves making a lot of choices based on it – the frequency, content, visual and verbal appeal, etc. If you ask young people, many will agree that they buy 'phones, laptops, shoes, clothes, etc. based on advertisement; sometimes it is from the recommendation of their peers.

The above takes us to what and who we love, and who we look down on. Occasionally, it is not based on objective reasoning. We may, therefore, like what our friends like, and follow who the group follows; contrariwise, we tend to despise people and products that close people we trust have similar negative opinion or sentiments against.

How do you react to who God despises? Would you see and accept His point of view that even a *mighty hero* (verse 1) who is <u>also</u> boastful, deceitful and destructive, should be despised the way God sees them, as a disgrace? It may be difficult to understand this verse since the rest of the world may applaud them. The hero may not be a globally-known person, but just national, or in a community. At whatever level, a hero makes themselves and is also made by the community. It means that the person has met the criterion for qualification as a hero. Many people are intelligent, wealthy, etc. but not so many are heroes. A boastful hero is like a person who blows trumpet for themselves; for people who have class, that is disgraceful. It is really despicable to God.

CHAPTER 31

The Lot of Those Who Trust the Lord

Psalm 52: 6–9

The lot, or destiny, of people who put their trust in God is very different from that of people who do otherwise. The funny thing is that even though people are either watchful or have lived for a long time their keen observations or what they have learnt from the experiences of other people do not seem to serve them well; this is because they repeat others' mistakes.

It appears that the things that God allows to happen in the lives of both wicked and righteous people is to make people learn and therefore desist from wrong practices, and adopt right ways of living. Verses 6 and 7 refer to the lot of the person who trusted in their immense wealth rather than trust in God, and also grew strong by decimating others. We still find such people in various communities – in particular the suddenly-rich men and women with questionable means of wealth acquisition in poor countries. We are not referring to those who gain their wealth by legitimate means and use the wealth to add value to their society. The ones who gain wealth by ungodly means destroy other people actually or figuratively. They may destroy the lives of entire families by refusing to pay the salaries of committed employees who work for them in their various enterprises; other times the high level of corruption they engage in destroys the economies of their countries, and they do not care that present and future generations will suffer from their avarice. God has a way of bringing down, snatching, plucking and uprooting them, verse 5. We see it or watch on TV.

The lot of those who trust God is different. They are useful to their societies like the olive tree is to humankind, and will forever flourish in God's presence – verse 8. They feel confident in God's presence. One of the reasons that those that trust God are confident in the presence of people and God is that they hope in God's good name, verse 9 (see also Proverbs 18:10); they can praise God at all times and have no reason to watch their backs.

CHAPTER 32

How God Sees Foolishness

Psalm 53: 1–6

You will notice that verse 1 of this psalm does not say that foolish people say out that there is no God. What it says is that the fool *says in his heart* that there is no God. There could be some reasons that make them not say it out. One could be that if just thinking and believing that there is no God is foolishness, saying it to the hearing of people would be gross foolishness. The other reason could be that the fool does not have to say it but act it. The Bible tells us that as a person thinks in their heart so they are – Proverbs 23: 7. We can extend this to the fool and say that as a fool thinks in their heart so they are. They will, consequently, behave like fools. And what does God say the fool practices (or is like)?

The following is a list of the characteristics of fools as indicated in verses 1—4 of this passage:

They are corrupt – Because they are corrupt, they distort facts and do crooked things. They thrive in warped minds, thoughts, actions and systems. When things are straight and proper, they feel uncomfortable there – and could actually attack such good conditions.

Their ways are vile – They are not disturbed about doing detestable or foul things. Don't you sometimes wonder why some people do awful things and think nothing about them? It is because the vile way is their way. Such people need prayers and God's intervention in their lives.

They have turned away – The people under this description have left the once right paths, and entered wrong paths. Either deliberately, or from confusion of the mind, what is wrong is now acceptable to them – as long as they are making outward progress.

They know nothing – Why would God use this expression? So, their high academic attainment, without acknowledging God, is knowing nothing? Since these people think in their hearts that there is no God, they do not know God – they cannot. People who do not know God really know nothing – whatever they know is futile to their eternity though it may be useful to them and the society on the basis of the temporal.

They never call on God – Yes, they cannot call on God because they have no right to do so. Those who turned away have lost whatever right they had to call on and relate with God. They are overwhelmed with dread even when there is, or should be, none; they are despised by God.

CHAPTER 33

Having Triumph Over Your Foes

Psalm 54: 1–7

It is an act of God to allow us to be alive and witness our victory over our foes, verse 7. It is of note that it is God who saves, vindicates and delivers us. He saves and vindicates us from our enemies, as well as delivers us from all manner of troubles.

In the context of this passage, we may see God saving us as preventing the plans of the enemy from happening, and/or bringing us out of their evil plots. In the case of vindication, God allows the truth to become evident; whereas an evil report may have been made about you or me behind our backs, God allows the truth of the case to be known to all, therefore acquitting us of the false accusations. But we must make sure that we do the right things to qualify for vindication.

With respect to deliverance we want to see it as one actually entering the trap of the enemy, but God bringing us out of it for His name's sake, and for our welfare. When God does the above, and other things, on our behalf we cannot but find ourselves watching this 'movie' about ourselves. We may watch it with surprise, relief, joy or a combination of them.

Our own part is to pray to God because God will listen and hear, verse 2. But how many times do we find ourselves wanting, simply because we are not alert and so may not even pray aright?

The other responsibility or duty is for us to praise God – it is interesting to praise God for His attributes (who He is) as well as for what He is yet to do. We tend to be more efficient with thanksgiving – which refers to our expressing gratitude for what God has done already. Whether we are praising the Lord or just thanking Him, or presenting our prayer requests to Him, we shall receive victory over our foes. But we *must not be* our own foes – for many are actually their own foes, while spending useful time looking for the enemy that is outside. If you discover that you are your own foe, you must overcome your bad attitudes, beliefs and actions.

CHAPTER 34

Wishing for Wings of a Dove

Psalm 55: 1–8

Here is a king in great distress. King David expresses his real feelings to God. Many of us have a problem with that and, if possible, would feign boldness in the face of great assaults. What were this king's challenges? His enemies were threatening him, verse 3; they brought down suffering on him verse 3; they made him the target of their anger, verse 3. The challenges made him have the following feelings: troubled thoughts and feelings of distress, verse 2; pain and grief in his mind, verse 4; terrifying images of imminent death, verse 4 and overpowering feelings of fear, trembling and horror, verse 6.

You could be asking why a king should be in this kind of emotional and physical state, instead of immediately using military might to quash the assault from opposing elements in the country. King David was an unusual king; he tended to do things in ways different from those of other people, including royalty. He chose to have dealings with God and to act according to God's dictates.

At a point, we find King David wishing out loud how he could develop wings like the dove's, and fly away to have rest, verse 6. Have you ever found yourself almost completely surrounded by troubles that had no easy answers? Apart from prayer to God, that he knew was the primary reaction under such circumstances, he concluded that he needed a breathing space. What came to his mind was the desert where he would not hear the sounds of the threats of people like his own son, Absalom, and the crowd that Absalom had won over.

It is important to know that the problems of life do not skip anybody. Kings and queens, the peasant and the poor, all have their times of distress. We must realize that it is not every time that we are strong. May you and I have the correct responses when we are in the midst of unusual challenges. It may not be a wise thing to continue saying 'it is not my portion' as no one is spared.

CHAPTER 35

Unshakable When with God

Psalm 55: 16–23

The psalmist continues to describe his immense challenges and his responses. All of us find that there is at least once that we have experienced (or will experience) very difficult times. Even as a king, this writer made sure that he communed with God regularly for he said that he was crying aloud to God *in the evening, in the morning and at noon*, verse 17. He said that God rescued him unhurt even though a battle was waged against him. It did not matter that many people were opposed to him, verse 18.

Allegiance of men and women changes, and David found that even those who were friendly had turned around to be in the group of those that wanted his death, verse 20. They were deceitful and smooth-tongued, but he had seen them for who they really were. But the unchangeable friend and helper that we have is God, and King David proved Him to be so, verse 19. David compared his throne with God's and confirmed that unlike his throne that was subject to assault, God's throne was established from of old and He was seated on the throne unchangeably, verse 19. Because King David was aligned with this great God, he was confident that God heard both sides: his side and their side. In the same 19, he knew that God would *'humble them because they have no fear of God.'* I believe that when we cry to God in prayer, we must ensure that we are on the right track and have been doing what the Lord approves of. It is because he sees both sides. It is only when we have the mind and behavior of King David that God will humble our enemies who do not fear God.

It is when we ally with this unshakeable God that we too are unshakeable. We should just remember to cast our concerns on the Lord and be assured that He will sustain us, verse 22. Moreover, God will never let the righteous be shaken, verse 22. We praise God for this assurance. On your part and mine will we be able to say like this king, '*But as for me, I trust in you (God)*', verse 23?

CHAPTER 36

How to Handle Fear

Psalm 56: 1–13

The subject of this brief study is *fear* and, specifically, how to handle it. It may be worth the while to use the experience of King David as documented in this passage to show what made him fear and then imitate his solution to the experience of fear. When evil or danger is from afar, it is easier to gather support from people near you to handle it. However, when the cause of fear is very near, and virtually within your circle of operation, it becomes a more complicated matter. The latter was the experience of King David.

This king lived and ruled in the days when communication with people from distant places was not easy to achieve; the same thing applied to physical attacks from distant enemies as there were no war planes or fast-moving warships. He, therefore, had to contend with enemies who were so near that they could hear his words and twist them, verse 3; they could see him and watch his steps or actions to see how and when he would make mistakes and, perhaps, how they could take advantage of 'inside' information to hurt him and his throne, verse 6. These people were so close that they could plot against him all day, on a daily basis, without being spotted or suspected, verses 1 and 5. These were scary for him and remain scary for us today. We experience similar situations in the place of work, in our private businesses, and sometimes in our very homes.

The king had a solution. He said in verses 3 and 4: *"When I am **afraid**, I put my **trust** in you. ……. In God I **trust** and am not **afraid**."* The first use of *trust* is curative, and the second use of the same word is preventive.

Curative: When you find that fear has already taken hold of your heart, the way to go is to trust in God.

Preventive: When you put your trust in God firmly, that shield of faith (Ephesians 6:16) will not allow fear to penetrate and gain access into your mind and spirit.

We, therefore, see that we can use our Faith in God to both handle fear and to prevent it. It works both ways.

CHAPTER 37

Surviving in Hostile Environments

Psalm 57: 1–11

What manner of hostility would make the perpetrators be described as: Lions, ravenous beasts, having teeth akin to spears and arrows, having tongues like sharp swords? These are the expressions we find in verse 4. Nobody would choose to associate with such obviously vicious individuals. The writer, however, had no choice but to be in the midst of these people. Have you ever found yourself in an environment or circumstance where every time you turned around, you encountered people who were far from being friendly or helpful? Are you presently in a situation where the only things you want are peace and quietness, but what you find are confusion, opposition, misunderstanding or misrepresentation? These things did not start today and will very likely not end with you; this is simply because Satan is not dead, and he specializes in using human instruments who may not even realize that they are in his employ.

In this psalm, King David shows us *four strategies* that he used to survive in environments that were hostile. He documented them for our benefit. The very first strategy is in verse 4 where he said *'I am in the midst of lions ….'* This first strategy is *Correct assessment*. He did not deceive himself by wishing the bad situation away. Shouldn't we do likewise? The second strategy is recorded in verse 7; here he said *'My heart is steadfast.'*

Steadfastness or resoluteness is very important for it keeps you and me focused and at high alert in such situations. The third strategy is found in verse 8 where he awakens his soul, his harp and the dawn. These simply describe *Spiritual state of prayer and praise.* The last strategy is *Knowing that the disaster will pass*, verse 1. Wouldn't you rather use these strategies for your good? May you have God as your Refuge – verse 1.

CHAPTER 38

They Attacked Me
Without A Cause

Psalm 59: 1–11

It is amazing that the best king of Israel documented the words in this passage as his experiences. Then who is immune to these things? We all know that most people will make false declaration of their goodness or innocence, but David was not a man of that ilk; we know that he was not that type of person because of the unusually open confession of wrongdoing and guilt he made in Psalm 51. The king categorically stated in verse 4 that he did no wrong, yet they were ready to attack him. The king mentioned this category of people again in Psalm 69 where, in verse 4, he described them as *"Those who hate me without reason outnumber the hairs of my head; many are my enemies without cause, those who seek to destroy me."* These people were not there for jokes, but had a sinister assignment. Who were the *they*? They were his *enemies*, verse 1 and also *wicked traitors*, verse 5.

When this ugly situation takes place and you happen to be the target, what should you do? For many of us the initial reaction is denial, especially when the people are traitors – for traitors could have been friendly previously. Traitors are double-agents and may not be identified easily. Our second reaction is to go off the handle and, in a fit of rage, do something equally bad. The third natural reaction is to wish and actually pray for their death. What did King David do? He prayed to God for deliverance and watched out for Him to do it – verses 1, 2 and 9. He asked God to uproot them and bring them down, but not to kill them – verse 11.

You may wonder why David was so different from many of us. David had learnt over the years to identify closely with God. He was the same person who wrote, in Psalm 23, that God prepared a table before him in the presence of his enemies. Yes, David did not want those avowed enemies of his to die. If they died, they would not endure the pain and displeasure of being witnesses to the goodness of God in his life. Moreover, if they died, the living would forget the disgrace of David's enemies.

CHAPTER 39

Rock That Is Higher Than I

Psalm 61: 1–7

It is not part of human nature to give prominence to another person, over and above ourselves. Many of us may profess humility, but deep inside us self or ego is protected jealously, and will be projected at an opportune time. There are a few people who unquestionably placed another person on a pedestal higher than themselves; one good example is John the Baptist who said that Jesus took pre-eminence and was to be preferred to him – Luke 3:16.

King David rightly saw God as the Rock that was higher than him. As strong as he was, he found himself in a situation where his heart was faint – he was vulnerable and he knew it. He was a practical and truthful man. He asked to be taken *to the Rock that is higher than I.* What is your fortress or strong tower? We shall briefly mention two examples. In Proverbs 10:15 we read that *'The wealth of the rich man is his fortified city....'* and Proverbs 18:10 records, *'The name of the Lord is a fortified tower, the righteous run to it and are safe.'* King David was a righteous, rich and powerful man, yet he opted to have God as the Rock that was higher than he, and his strong tower against the foe.

This king further showed his desire to dwell in God's tent forever (verse 4), mimicking the expression in Psalm 23:6. In addition he craved the safety of the powerful protective 'wings' of God, same verse 4. It is obvious that these were King David's deep-seated, well-founded sentiments and belief, and not just religious expressions for people to hear. We know that there are many people who say they depend on God, but they actually depend on their wealth as well as spiritual, political, and business connections. May you be like King David.

CHAPTER 40

Trust in God: Not in People or Riches

Psalm 62:1–12

The beginning of this psalm describes the situation we find among so many people. These people are not happy that other people have attained lofty heights. The successful people referred to may be people who are very close or not so close to these people who are not happy, but may pretend to be happy. The heights attained may be high levels of financial success, professional height, spiritual prominence, educational attainment, political relevance, career status, etc.

For these people, it is not enough that they feel bad about the other person, but they go on to plan for or plot their downfall. The unfortunate thing is that the victim of this plot usually does not know the evil or bad plan against them because they cannot see the *heart* of the pretending, wicked person. Because they do not see the heart, they are likely to become easy prey, unless God is very much on their side.

The word of God tells us a very simple but profound truth – *"My salvation and my honor depend on God; he is my mighty rock, my refuge"*, verse 7. From this fact we should not put all our trust in people, but in God.

But, are we certain that the lofty height we have attained is an honor we received from God? As a person, ask yourself how you got to where you are. Was it through means which God would give approval to, or not? If, indeed, this honor depends on God, you do not have anybody or anything to fear, because God will be like a mighty rock and refuge for you. He will save you from human beings who tell lies and plan evil.

CHAPTER 41

God in My Meditation

Psalm 63:1–8

Many of us have had the experience of either finding it difficult to fall asleep, or having difficulty in getting back to sleep when we wake up long before our normal waking up time in the morning. There are reasons behind these two problems with sleep, but they are not part of this topic.

What do we do when it happens? People do some of the following: Take a hot or warm beverage to send them to sleep; take sleeping pills; read a novel with a pleasant story (not one that keeps the heart racing); make a telephone call to a friend, colleague, relation, or loved one even at odd hours; start an internet 'chat' with someone who is awake in a different time zone; wake up their partner and force a conversation; watch a movie; listen to music; start to write something or continue where they stopped; attend to office work they brought back home; look for something light to eat – and others. Another thing that people do is to pray; sometimes, they fall asleep, still kneeling down to pray.

Psalm 63:6 tells us*: "On my bed I remember you; I think of you through the watches of the night."* But we can only remember our Lord in the time of sleeplessness if verse 1 applies to us? It says: *".... earnestly I seek you; I thirst* *for you, my whole being longs for you,…."* We should seek God, desire for him whole-heartedly.

When we invite the Lord into what we do in the course of the day, week, month and year, it becomes easy to think of, or meditate on, God and His goodness to us when we are troubled at night. When we truly bring God into the picture and meditate, He will reassure us that He will *do it again.* His right hand upholds us *whether in the daytime or in the night hours,* verse 8. May you enjoy sleep as a beloved of the Lord.

When you are awake and fully aware of the watches (passing hours) of the night, there are the options of meditating on your pre-sleep problems/challenges or meditating on the Lord and His Word. Which one will you choose to meditate on?

CHAPTER 42

God Cares for Our Environment; So, Should I

Psalm 65:5–13

The psalmist says of God in the ninth verse: *"You care for the land and water it; you enrich it abundantly..."* Can that be said of human beings, you and me? How well do we care for our environment? The business God introduced Adam and Eve to in the book of Genesis can well be summarized as the business of caring for what God had created.

God's entire creation in terms of time and space, what we can see and what we cannot see because of size and distance; what we can smell, touch, feel, etc. is for us to care for. If all human beings appreciated what God created and took good care of them, our environment would be in proper balance and all of us would enjoy, the way God planned or ordained that we should. We, however, have the free will to choose to act the way we want, or in the way God wants us to. Even science has shown us that a lot of the ways we behave and the choices we make are harmful to us as individuals and a race, as well as harmful to the entire environment.

We and our God-given environment are intertwined, one, and inseparable. Let each of us retrace our steps, and care for our environment, rather than deplete and destroy it.

CHAPTER 43

Come and See

Psalm 66: 1–12

Parents love to make known what their children have done to make them proud; this is true right from the early childhood days, up to the time that they have their own families and achieve other things. In childhood, it may be talent in the arts, ability to do recitals or early signs of giftedness in acting, singing, etc. Later on, it could be the youngsters' abilities in sports, cooking, further improvement in sculpture, etc. Parents, friends, neighbors, school mates and school authorities all like to associate with success of children and young people. At college level, parents of the best graduating student share the glory at the convocation, or graduation ceremony. The whole idea is to make people *come and see*.

In this passage, the psalmist invites the reader to *come and see* the awesome things that God has made. He, therefore, showcases the handiwork of God. This psalm concentrates on the wonderful things that God has done for humankind, verse 5. Transforming the Red Sea into dry land to temporarily create a highway for His people to cross on foot remains an unmatched marvel, verse 6.

God ruling in power and watching the affairs of nations, are things that are difficult to understand; this is because it is frequently hard to comprehend how the behavior of world rulers, and the activities of human beings under their rule, fall into the plans and purposes of the Almighty. They, however, still fit in spite of appearing otherwise – these all show that He is an all-powerful God Who cannot be outsmarted, or taken by surprise. Because He does these inexplicable things, each of us can commit our lives and our affairs into God's hands, and be sure that what makes no sense in our lives can be transformed into great sense.

CHAPTER 44

Blessings and Harvest

Psalm 67: 1–7

Blessings and harvest are strongly related. The relationship is in the fact that without God blessing the work of our hands, there cannot be harvest. Harvest is just one of the numerous blessings that we get from God.

Making His face shine on us is one very important blessing from God, verse 1. His face shining on us is a favor, for should God consider the ways of humankind at any time in history what we deserve from Him are punishment, and scolding, at the least.

Another blessing that we find in this psalm is God ruling over humanity with equity, verse 4. Every reader should ponder over this truth, because equity or justice refers to fairness. Aside from favor, God deals with human beings on the basis of equity. This is why He will not bless the work of a lazy Christian, but will give abundant blessings to a non-Christian who, knowingly or unknowingly, obeys the injunction that we should work hard, conscientiously and sensibly; we must present to God the work of our hands for Him to bless – see Psalm 90:17.

Harvest suggests planting or sowing. We must ensure that we sow what is appropriate and good so that our harvest will be a bounty of what is good. We must realize that the same principles of sowing and harvesting pertaining to cultivating land apply to other forms of sowing. You should remember what the apostle Paul said viz.: *'Do not be deceived: God cannot be mocked. A man reaps what he sows'*, Galatians 6:7 and *'…. if any would not work, neither should he eat'*, 2 Thessalonians 3:10. To get the blessings, follow the rules. Sadly, the sowing and reaping law operates with the bad and ugly, the way it holds true for the good. In Hosea 8:7 we read: *They sow the wind and reap the whirlwind.* Human beings must take into consideration that evil also grows by multiplication, and not just by addition. It is, therefore, essential to depart from sowing evil; if a person does not, the harvest may come many-fold and, sometimes, so long after sowing took place that the connection is not obvious.

CHAPTER 45

Enemies of God

Psalm 68: 1–6

Does it not sound ridiculous that some people would make themselves enemies of God? Could it be that they are enemies of God and do not realize it? It is a known fact that some naïve persons have found themselves in very deep trouble and shown regrets following their naivety, carelessness, or both. These are people who collect parcels and even luggage from unscrupulous known or unknown persons and travel abroad with them only to find that they were trafficking in drugs. At the point of being discovered and arrested, they are enemies of the country where they are apprehended – whether they intended it or not, knew it or not.

People who are enemies of God find themselves in an awkward position, as they have nobody to appeal to. Moreover, their indiscretion or choices could have eternal consequences, unless they get a reprieve from the same God. Thankfully, God has made provision for that, by the sacrifice of Jesus Christ that makes it possible for God's enemies to be reconciled to God. No-one could put it more succinctly than the apostle Paul who said '...*Be reconciled to God*', 2 Corinthians 5:20.

But despite the above appeal from Jesus Christ through the apostle Paul, some people will remain stiff-necked and rather be like smoke that is dispersed by the wind or candle wax that is converted to liquid by the heat of fire; neither of them serves any useful purpose for long, and are actually consumed into irrelevance over time. Whoever chooses to oppose God is doing so temporarily, but the consequences to that person could be eternal damnation.

CHAPTER 46

Folly, Pain and Shame

Psalm 69: 1–6

None of the words in the title of this chapter is good. Folly can lead to pain and shame. Pain can make some people engage in acts that those who do not experience their level of pain may not understand – we see this in some women who undergo normal labor without receiving any form of pain reduction. On its own, shame from an act carried out by a friend, family member, school mate, etc. can cause emotional pain and suffering to other people.

The psalmist acknowledged his *folly* in verse 5. The action, word or belief that shows this folly is not stated. It is instructive that in the same verse he said that God was aware of the folly, and he felt guilty about it. If you find yourself in the shoes of this psalmist, may you feel concerned the way he felt – for, in doing so, there is hope that the folly will not be repeated.

In earlier verses he found himself in an embarrassing condition whereby he was like a drowning man; his catastrophe took place in deep waters that reached his neck, with no sign of a foothold to support him, verses 1 and 2. This is a *shameful* condition, but his reaction was appropriate for we read in verse 3 that he looked for and called on God. It pays to have the presence of mind to do that.

The last sad condition of this psalmist is *pain*. It is painful to find that you are hated without any reason, and your adversaries are not only many but also people close to you. It is even more painful if you have to go through what this psalmist experienced – being forced to restore what he did not steal, all in verse 4. Then would he be considered a thief by onlookers, to the shame of other God-fearing people who knew him to be a godly man.

CHAPTER 47

Weathering the Storm of Scorn

Psalm 69: 7–15

Nobody likes to be scorned. Not even children like it. You belittle a person when you scorn them. Such disrespect may stay in a person's mind long after the scorn. We know that a person can be scorned in writing, in speech, by action or even by mannerism. Of the listed ways of scorning someone the one that can be very subtle is gesture; this is because, while other people may understand the mannerism, the target of scorn may not have noticed it – and may not have understood it even if they noticed it.

The writer of this psalm stated very early in the psalm that he endured scorn for the sake of God, verse 7. This could be because he was doing something on behalf of God or the Gospel of Christ. This has happened to any Christian who has given out tracts or the New Testament to people. People reject the offer outright. Other people collect it and keep it aside and continue doing what they were doing – or if they were doing nothing, find something to pretend to be occupied with. Scorn is even more unbearable when it comes from members of one's family –verse 8. This could be because you continue seeing them or communicating with them and that reminds you of the scorn. This psalmist gave us two strategies for enduring scorn: One is that he saw it as a necessity, a thing that he had to bear; for, in verse 10 it is recorded *'I must endure scorn.'* When scorn has to do with your faith, the strategy is zeal; in verse 9, we read *'for zeal for your house consumes me.'* So, *acceptance* and *zeal* are two ways to endure scorn.

CHAPTER 48

In Emergency, Call 911

Psalm 70: 1–5

Just like in our day-to-day activities, issues may arise that fall into the class of emergency; the day suddenly changes for whoever experiences them. In an emergency, the most logical and instinctive thing to do is to call the emergency help line, 911. But to call the number, certain assumptions must have been made and they must be right. It should be unheard of that 911 was called and there was no call pick-up; it is also an impossibility that only one person will be on duty when multiple calls could come in; it would also be wrong to be unable to call 911 because of financial constraint on the part of the caller.

Something similar to the above also happens in our spiritual lives. You cannot be in a serious trouble and yet you are not sure that God you are calling hears, will listen and accept to do something. It is because we know that when we are in emergency situations, God will answer that we are fully persuaded to call on Him. God even encourages us to do so for we read in Psalm 50:15 that we should call on God in the day of trouble and He will rescue us.

Verses 1 and 5 give us all the ingredients of calls in such emergencies. There are three, and are: *Who to call, the Content of the call and How the response should be.* The Person to call is God – and we have direct access to Him in the sense that there is no human being to screen calls and determine whether to let them go through. The content of the call is simply 'Help and Save.' How the response should come is 'Quickly and Without delay.'

CHAPTER 49

A Wonder to Many People

Psalm 71:1–8

The psalmist hereby tells us things about his life vis-à-vis God. He tells of the past and present with the past being his testimonies and the present being the objects of his prayer. If a person who does not understand the ways of God goes through some of the experiences of this man, you will observe that they will be whining and even blaming God. You must take notice that this psalm is like a brief curriculum vitae or biodata of the writer. It commences from his birth for he says in verse 6 that it was God who brought him out from his mother's womb. Many doctors and nurses that have attended to pregnant women in labor recognize the fact that some labor does not culminate in normal delivery but in assisted instrumental delivery which may be operative i.e. by caesarean section. You can imagine that a baby born after difficult labor or by operation will appreciate that it was by God's grace that they came out of the mother's womb. This does not suggest that this song writer experienced these things because even normal delivery is an act that God built into us.

In verse 5 he mentions that God had been his help and confidence since his youth. What are you doing with your youth, or what have you been doing since your youth – if you have passed the stage of youth? In the rest of the verses the psalmist tells God that He was his rock, fortress and place of refuge, and prayed to Him to give the command for his salvation from ruthless people. He ended the song by telling God that his mouth was filled with praises for God's splendor on a daily basis.

He could not end his testimonies and prayers without observing that God had made him to be like a wonder, or sign, to many observers. When you are a wonder to many, it reflects the fact that God has basically turned you into a living testimony; a testimony that amazes people, either in the quality of happenings pertaining to you, or in the great numbers in which they occur. While the story ends well, the journey must have been very rough and traumatic.

CHAPTER 50

Understand When Others Don't

Psalm 71:9–17

It is interesting that things do happen in a person's life and they can neither relate them all nor even begin to fathom how and why they happen; yet there are unfriendly watchers who seem to know it all. These are the people who give wrong or warped explanations for those occurrences. They do not bother themselves with the great and marvelous things that happen in your life but will proffer explanations for each and every sad thing that comes into your life. This may be why the psalmist here humbly stated that he would mention God's saving acts in his life *'though I know not how to relate them all',* verse 15; but we also read in verse 11 that his enemies said *"God has forsaken him;"* Is it not interesting or sad (depending on how you view it) that it is not friends, but enemies who believe that they are qualified to know what is happening in the life of a person – and, in this case, a Christian or godly person?

Every experienced Christian knows that the fact that God is in their lives does not mean that sad, negative and unwanted things will not happen to them. Even the heroes of faith in the Old Testament knew that; we have a good example in Joseph who experienced sibling betrayal, sale into slavery, and false imprisonment – and yet he understood them, Genesis 50:20. In the New Testament, the apostle Paul indicated that he suffered all manner of things, including shipwreck thrice, treachery, and betrayal from those close to him, 2 Corinthians 11:25, 26. He understood it as part of his work of spreading Christ's good news. These faithful believers understood even when others could not. What of you?

CHAPTER 51

Choosing Between Honor and Shame

Psalm 71:18–24

The choice between honor and shame should be obvious, but in real life we find that it is not. Otherwise, how do you explain the innumerable situations where intelligent, successful and prominent individuals do things that can only be described as shameful? In isolated cases, one could explain away their actions, words or behavior as accidental or simply slips. When they are recurrent and assume a predictable pattern, it can only be a choice. People who engage in shameful acts have actually chosen them, and either ignored or jettisoned honor.

It is from the place of honor that a person who has seen many troubles classified as 'bitter', attributes them to God (verse 20), and still goes on to tell the same God from their heart of hearts that He is righteous and unique (verse 19). Honorable people respect themselves, and hold other people in high regard – unless the latter are despicable people, in which case extolling them would be ridiculous to any onlooker. Honorable people see the hand of God in their lives. Honorable people put their hope and trust in God, like this psalmist did, looking beyond happenings in their lives to the One Who is in control of the happenings, verse 20b. Honorable people have the future in mind, and they desire to leave behind a good legacy; consequently, they actively educate the 'next generation' on God's power and mighty acts (verse 18), to enable them see the relevance of the Almighty in their lives, verse 18.

People who do otherwise have actually chosen shame; we continue seeing it in the lives of many people. Our prayer is that you and I will not be in this category. Amen.

CHAPTER 52

Godly Leaders Harness Wealth for All

Psalm 72:1–7, 12–15

How will God "Endow the king with 'His' justice (and) righteousness" if the sovereign refuses to relate to God as a son or daughter? How many 'kings' in low places like leaders in government offices, educational institutions, private organizations, local government and similar-level councils are willing to submit to God as children would submit to a father? When we consider individuals that occupy posts in higher levels, like state or regional governors, ambassadors, ministers, senate and house of assembly, or house or representatives and similar-level leaders, do they do better? And those at the very top like national leaders – presidents, prime ministers, etc. are they ready to take God as a father? Until that happens, leadership shall not be with clear-cut justice and righteousness – doing the right no matter how costly and unpopular it is.

Governments or leaders should harness the wealth in natural resources, like mountains and hills, the land and sea, for the people. They should also provide security and safety for the society. Government should use its power to have and use institutions to protect the weak and the vulnerable from the powerful.

Don't we see those exploited without recourse to justice and any form of fair treatment outside the judicial system? How precious is the blood of citizens to their elected leaders? This passage rings true in every corner of the earth; some parts of the globe are doing well and others are not doing well at all.

All leaders should know that if they chose to lead and serve well, their followers would pray *May he endure as long as the sun, as long as the moon, through all generations,* verse 5. It is a wonderful privilege to be a leader anywhere in the world. When leaders in poor countries and communities do what is right, gold will pursue them, and they will stop pursuing gold senselessly. We pray that as you have opportunity to lead, you will do better than leaders (past and present) who have missed the right way, and also lost the opportunity of being instruments for implementing God's plans for their people.

CHAPTER 53

Yes, Wicked People Do Prosper

Psalm 73: 1–9

We all know that money has a special place in the history of humankind. Money has taken many forms – from trade by barter, to manila, to coins, to various types of paper, and to cashless forms; this is not necessarily the correct order of transition, or evolution of money. Money has been a tool used to measure wealth, though wealth or prosperity is not synonymous with money. For this write-up we also consider things like intelligence, beauty, talent, etc. as types of wealth. A very brilliant professional may not necessarily be the person that earns the highest amount of monetary income.

We also know that money could be indiscriminate in who it gets attracted to. The Bible tells us in Ecclesiastes 10:19 that *"…But money answers everything"* NKJV. It is, therefore, not surprising that money can be used to address the good, the bad, or the ugly. And if that is the case, should it be surprising that money can answer to the righteous and unrighteous, the wicked and the good? No. We therefore boldly state that 'Yes, wicked people do prosper.'

"The prosperity of the wicked", verse 3, can appear very attractive and enviable. Why not? Read this passage and the entire chapter and you will

find the way the psalmist described the owners of such prosperity: They seem to lack nothing, as things seem to go well with them in virtually every area of life. They even imagine and speak audacious things – up to the extent of believing that they are the owners of not just the earth but heaven also, verse 9. But this prosperity is deceitful – see verses 18–20.

CHAPTER 54

God Despises Them as Fantasies

Psalm 73: 10–12, 18–20

It is because they do not seem to have any care in the world like normal human beings that there is a tendency for crowds to get attracted to wicked prosperous people. Their bad character and actions are easily relegated to the background – like they do not exist, though day-in and day-out the same prosperous people wreak a lot of havoc on people. The closeness in relationship that people have with them does not matter to them as we sometimes find that wicked prosperous people are vicious even to their parents, spouses, siblings, and children. Verse 10 states this situation clearly and briefly.

Many wicked prosperous people sometimes actually get to the point where they believe that God does not see what they do to get their wealth, or to maintain it. The way they spend money could also destroy many other families and communities as they occasionally use their financial wealth to coerce youths and not-so-well-endowed adults to do things the latter would ordinarily not want to do. In the minds of such prosperous people, does God know anything, even though He is the Highest? – verse 11.

Unfortunately for them, God places them on slippery ground and we frequently bear witness to their downfall and ruin, sometimes suddenly, verse 18. In the eyes of God, though those who respect them feel otherwise, they are like a dream when a dreamer awakes. How do you feel when you have a pleasant, vivid dream and then wake up only to confirm that it was actually a dream? Moreover, to their admirers they are the *real thing*, but God dismisses them as fantasies – verse 20.

CHAPTER 55

The Owner of Day and Night

Psalm 74: 16–23

God is the Owner of both day and night. The day and night are the primary instruments that humans use to determine time. If our lives consisted of continuous daytime or continuous night time, it would be almost impossible to easily know that one day has passed and another emerged.

It is actually true that God has built into humankind systems in our bodies that respect day and night. Some parts of our bodies recognize the day and night and function when they are supposed to function, and rest when they are supposed to rest, for optimal effectiveness of the human body. Animals are not different, for God has done it in such a way that some of them work best in the daylight hours, while others do so in darkness. The summary of the matter is that, in God's goodness and grace, He divided a full day into two important parts – day and night – and this division is not arbitrary, but a demonstration of His immense wisdom.

Verses 16 and 17 of this Psalm inform us that God established the sun and moon, set boundaries for the earth, and also created summer and winter. He did the same for parts of the world that essentially have two seasons – rainy and dry. We find that the sun, moon, land and water boundaries, and the seasons **all** know their functions, abide by them and obey God's will concerning them – and they have been doing so right from creation.

It is only humankind that fall short of God's plans, as we have failed woefully in our responsibility of honoring God in worship and caring for the rest of His creation; He gave us the unique duty of overseeing God's entire 'estate' on His behalf, verses 18–23. God did not ask humans to prey on themselves but to live in harmony. The wicked among us behave like they are the owners of all, with the right to destroy at will – but God remains the maker and owner of all, including the day and night.

CHAPTER 56

Limitations for The Brave

Psalm 76: 1–6

There is no community or country that does not relish in its valiant citizens – both men and women. Many of these brave citizens are a gift to places where they come from in times of crises or preparation for difficult times and situations. It is because of this that leaders of governments that plan well for their countries ensure that they not only have a strong military force consisting of the army, navy and air force, but also gather the very best from these arms of the military to create an elite group. This special force is indeed a gem to their countries, and they execute special assignments that others may not be able to do, or even attempt.

In human terms, the people and group mentioned above are the ultimate, and if a problem is beyond them it means that the problem should be studied specially and a strategy found to give to them to apply. In this psalm, we read of limitations for the brave. In the age when this psalm was written, the brave used arrows, shields and swords as their weapons of war – verse 3. You can easily deduce that arrows are weapons of attack, shields are weapons of defense, and swords play a dual role – for offense and defense. When properly used, these basic weapons for direct land battle were indispensable to brave soldiers; they were so indispensable that an army with horses and chariots could easily be routed without them.

They, however, would find themselves helpless dealing with an Opponent that uses light as a weapon. How do you fight against light, knowing that light is all around you and is not flesh and blood, verse 4? So why don't the valiant know that God is their ruin, verse 6? This topic may make a reader feel that the contents have no bearing with them. We, however, know that there are many people whose belief system and behavior are worse than these valiant men's and women's; they are the ones who, in their daily lives, forget that God is all around them like light is around them. They, therefore, in boldness, pursue ventures and practices that God clearly says *no* to. Their limitation remains God.

CHAPTER 57

God's Judgment Favors
the Afflicted

Psalm 76: 7–12

In many modern communities, indigenes, visitors, and foreigners do not know some of the traditional values of the people. Some of these values have always been good; others that were adjudged to be good have been found to be bad, based on current knowledge. Two good examples are killing of twins that Mary Slessor remains a heroine for combating; the other is fattening young women in preparation for marriage – which, today, is unacceptable and recognized as adverse to health, since obesity is known to be a risk factor for hypertension, etc.

But it is amazing that young and not-so-young people today have no respect for traditional values that have always been good; they even go further to show no regard for judgment passed by community elders against the guilty on such cases. The disregard takes the form of continuing with the negative practices, or refusing to pay the token penalty for such acts. In larger communities, with a good representation of multiple ethnicities, people tend to jettison their good traditional values and go further to adopt the adverse traditional practices of other ethnic groups!

What is described above holds because laws of many countries are comprehensive, covering every geographical area, without necessarily addressing the minutiae in every community or ethnic group in the country. The people who flout local traditional rules would not dare to break the general law, because they know that there are provisions in the law to apprehend such people and commit them to jail.

This write-up concentrates on God's opinion on the afflicted. There is a Judge whose area of jurisdiction is the whole world; He is the Highest God. He is the only one to be feared and nobody can stand before Him when He is angry, verse 7. We read in Hebrews 10:31 that it is not pleasant, but *fearful*, to fall into God's hands. When people afflict the helpless, they must remember that their judge is this same angry God who is feared by even kings who have encountered Him, verses 7 and 12.

CHAPTER 58

Questions During Sleepless Nights

Psalm 77: 1–9

Adults who, week-in and week-out, consistently sleep through the night hours peacefully without any form of sleep interruption, may not realize how privileged or blessed they are. Another name for sleeplessness is insomnia. Insomnia has many causes, but when it comes to the way it disturbs people it may simply be seen as one in which a person finds it difficult to start to sleep; for other people initiation of sleep is not a problem, but the sleep is for only very few hours – like between two and four hours; yet for other people they fall asleep and wake up frequently; and other people tend to sleep for many hours but when they wake up they feel almost as tired as when they fell asleep.

From the above description you can fill in the gaps with your imagination of what happens to anyone who finds themselves in any of the scenarios listed above. The psalmist described a personal case – and we do not know whether it was a one-off experience, or it was a common occurrence. When you read verses 6–9 what you find is a series of questions, totaling six. Questions bordered on: 1. God rejecting him; 2. Fear of no more favor from God; 3. Loss of unfailing love; 4. Doubt about God's promise; 5. Wondering about God's mercy, and 6. God withholding His compassion from him. These are questions that passed through (and, maybe, continued to play over-and-over in) the mind in one night – but this sleeper's desire was to sleep and not to keep thinking. And one can also imagine that the questions could have been more, with these six being the ones documented!

So, what do you do in such cases? The answer is in verses 1, 2 and 6: Cry out to God in prayer for help, remember and sing appropriate songs and stretch out 'untiring hands' to God. At the beginning, those untiring hands were because he would not be comforted, but might those same untiring hands not have been stretched out, by verse 6, in praise? Are you willing and ready to transit from despair to praise, the way this psalmist did? It is possible to praise God even in adverse circumstances.

CHAPTER 59

Investing in Our Children

Psalm 78: 1–8

Many parents limit their investment in their children to providing them with intellectual needs (in the form of a good education), and physical needs. These are good and it is important to remind Christian parents, that there is another crucial responsibility that God has placed on us but, unfortunately, many of us ignore it completely or pay scant attention to it; the negligible attention yields results that sometimes shock the parents.

This duty is to make our children grow in the grace and in the knowledge of our Lord and Savior Jesus Christ, 2 Peter 3: 18, and to ensure that we help our children grow not only in 'knowledge' and 'stature', but also in favor with God and man – the way our Lord Jesus grew as documented in Luke 2: 52. There is no real point in a child growing up to be a very highly educated, physically imposing, healthy and strong adult, and yet be a nuisance in the society and have no regard for God. It is unfortunate, but true, that such people have sprung up not only from families of parents who were not really interested in God and the Christ, but also from committed Christians who were 'spiritually asleep' when the spiritual enemy (i.e. the devil) worked in the lives of their children imperceptibly but certainly.

The good news is that it is not late to start doing the right thing even now – as long as you are committed to continue doing it. Let us pass godly information on to our children and future generations and show them how to put their trust in God and not forget His deeds, verse 7.

I consider it sad that the church of today is generally guilty of ignoring some critical Old Testament truth and practices that would have catapulted us and our children to marvelous spiritual and social heights, like what we find in Psalm 78, and rather emphasized other areas to a point of skew – yet those selected, apparently outwardly beneficial points have taken us nowhere, in terms of God's unchangeable priorities for His people. It is not late for us to change, wherever we have been faulted.

CHAPTER 60

Meet Your Burden Remover

Psalm 81: 1–9

In verses 5 and 6 this psalmist wrote: "I heard an unknown voice say: *I removed the burden from their shoulders; their hands were set free from the basket.*" The account in this psalm refers to ancient Israel as the people suffered in captivity in Egypt. You will remember that in Genesis they entered Egypt as celebrities but became slaves for over 400 years, and it was only with a mighty arm – one much mightier than that of the Pharaoh at the time – that God delivered the children of Israel through the instruments of Moses and Aaron.

The Unknown voice is certainly that of God. The words *shoulders, hands,* and *basket* are used to represent where the burden hurt (shoulders), what lifted the burden from the ground (hands) and the vehicle or container of the burden (basket). Certainly, as long as an object is on the ground it is not a burden to the ground or anyone – the most that it can be is an obstacle. But physical obstacles are separated from the human body and only prevent a person from getting to where they want, unless they are surmounted.

A burden is worse, as it is a burden because it is on a person's body. It increases the bodyweight and could present a very serious limitation to the burden carrier. Why then would another person want to lift or remove the burden, if not at least because of pity for the bearer? To carry another person's burden for them, there has to be something higher than just concern and pity – this is caused by **love** for the erstwhile burden carrier. But Jesus did it for us for the LORD laid on Him our iniquity as a group, Isaiah 53: 6.

We cannot replicate what Jesus did for humankind. Nevertheless, Jesus expects us to reduce each other's pain by carrying each other's burdens, see Galatians 6: 2; this does not mean encouraging self-inflicted burdens – go slightly down to verse 5. Understanding and doing what Jesus wants in this matter is one way to fulfil the law of Christ, which really is love, John 13: 35.

CHAPTER 61

Mouthful of Satisfaction

Psalm 81: 10–16

This psalm is worth reading over and over. The reason is because it seems to place the quality of our present and future in our hands, no matter what we did with our past. We know that some people who made right choices in the past, sadly drifted from them along the line and today their experience is very different when compared with their past. Similarly, other people, for one reason or the other, made horrible choices, 'got burnt', learnt from the consequences and made a U-Turn, and today the bad experiences remain where they deserve – the past. We conclude that it is a matter of choice. But we find ourselves making choices virtually on a daily basis; it is instructive that a bad one could spell disaster just as a good one may translate us into higher realms in any respect – health, career, marriage, finance, etc.

In this psalm God emphasized use of just three parts of our bodies: our mouths, ears and feet/legs. In verse 10 God told Israel to *open their mouth wide* and He would fill it. What enters our mouths affects our lives positively or negatively. But God feeds us with good food only. What God asked them to do was much easier than the effort of a new-born baby to eat. In verses 11 and 13 the next requirement was for Israel to just use their ears and *listen to Him* for instructions and guidance. Lastly, we read in verse 13 that they were to simply *follow in His ways* – meaning that since God knew the way, He would go in front of them. But what happened? In each case Israel refused. They did not open their mouth, listen to God or follow Him.

Is this not what many of us are still doing today? We say we are God's children but simple, direct instructions from God Himself are considered suspicious by us. Why so simple? We want to do difficult things, perhaps to 'impress' God? God goes on to ask us to listen, but we block our ears and preferentially listen to other sources. He is in front, asking us to follow – yet we say, no! Note that in verse 16, God reminded them that their obedience would lead to mouthful of satisfaction – with wheat and honey. That promise holds true today, for the obedient.

CHAPTER 62

'Gods' That Will Die
Like Mere Mortals

Psalm 82: 1–8

This psalmist gives us very sobering thoughts about judges and their responsibility of listening to cases and giving judgment. Here judges are referred to as *gods*. This means that in this psalm the word *god* does not refer to idols, but rather to judicial officers called judges. In various parts of the world, they also bear the name magistrates, and magistrates usually handle cases that are lower than the ones that judges adjudicate on. Before we continue it is important to realize that the following are the things that God said about judges.

That:

a. God is actually the one who presides in the great assembly where cases are heard, considered, and judgment is passed. This means that whenever they sit in the court house, judges must realize that they should represent God seeing that He is in their midst – whether known or unknown to them, verse 1;

b. They should stop defending the unjust and granting favors to the wicked, verse 2;

c. They should defend the weak and fatherless, maintain the rights of the poor and oppressed, and rescue the needy and weak. Simply put, they should always do what is fair and right to everybody, verses 3 and 4;

d. They should stop behaving like the ignorant and blind, who are unqualified to judge, verse 6.

Being a judge is being an occupier of a privileged position. Theirs is such a high post that it is reminiscent of the position of God. God is just, and a judge must be just. A judge must realize that the responsibility placed on them is almost sacred. They actually have the power of life and death (for certain crimes that people commit, classified as capital), just as they have the authority to sentence a suspect to jail or to set another free, based on the demerit or merit of the particulars of the case. A judge must not think in terms of pecuniary benefits or material acquisition – they could leave their position and become businessmen or businesswomen, if they become interested in and focused on money. God reminded them that though He is the One who called them 'gods' they should realize they would die like mere mortals.

CHAPTER 63

Even the Sparrow

Psalm 84: 1–4, 10–12

Even the sparrow and the swallow, two small birds, find shelter in the house of God. Whether it was the temple or tabernacle, they found their way there. Nobody stopped them, just like nobody would successfully stop them today in a church building – unless great effort is made. If the swallow can find its way to the house of God, why would a human being have difficulty going to church today? These birds went to the house of God even though the temple was not built for them.

In our own case the temple was built for people, and today churches are built for people too. In our time, and in many countries, there are people who do not go to church – and when they go, they do so on special occasions like Christmas, New Year, Palm Sunday, Good Friday and Easter, or for a friend's or relation's wedding, baby baptism/dedication, etc. For the latter religious-cum-social events, some people even wait until the church service is over, then go straight from their homes for the reception part of the ceremonies. Yes, even the sparrow and swallow *go to church* and desire to live there without paying rent. Sparrows desire to live there and the swallow even thinks of its babies and prepares room for them too by constructing a nest in God's house. They, therefore, want something more lasting or permanent – but many people do not take pleasure in going to church at all these days.

But why do some people develop an aversion for going to church? We who go to church and the leadership of churches would do well to ask this question and find answers. Could it be that what people observe in our lives outside church and what is taught in church are different? Is it message, hearer or messenger that hurts?

It will be good for each reader to consider the truth that the house of God is a representation of *the presence of God*. If you are uncomfortable with a physical structure called church building, have you considered the reality that you are still in the presence of God, including when you ignore Him and stay away from church?

CHAPTER 64

Listening to God

Psalm 85: 1, 2, 8–13

Doubtless, you know that there is a difference between hearing and listening. There are many times you sit in your house and hear the sound of vehicular traffic, yet pay scant attention to it. The fact that you give little regard to the sound is that it is of no real value to you – consequently, though you hear, you do not listen. If, however, you hear a sudden loud noise, you will suspend whatever you are doing and listen to the sound to determine whether it denotes a burst tire or a gunshot.

We do a similar thing with matters pertaining to God – and sometimes with God. We hear the Word of God but we do not *listen*. We listen to Christian music, love the tune but do not listen to the lyrics; when we listen to the lyrics we may not consider the exact meaning – and, since we did not get the meaning, we let opportunities for applying the truth of the music or messages we listened to earlier in the day, the previous day or month to slip by.

In verse 8, this psalmist said that he would listen to what God said. What God said at that time is the same thing He is still saying; and the way the writer listened is the way we should listen, if we are to get maximum benefits from God's sayings. As you read the rest of this psalm you will observe that it mentions promises and conditions. We shall consider just one pair which is in the same verse 8: God promised (and still promises) peace to His people on the condition that they do *not turn to folly.*

It actually pays to listen to what God says. Even Christians who are very committed to church and the activities therein, sometimes get so familiar with God and His sayings that they do not really listen to Him. Many, for example, have claimed wonderful promises, without paying attention to the detail that the promises come with conditions – as in verses 8 and 13. In verse 13, righteousness is the condition. <u>You meet the conditions before God's promises become yours</u>. Don't some people in otherwise blessed, peaceful, advanced countries turn to folly e.g. gun violence in peace times?

CHAPTER 65

When People Have No Regard for God

Psalm 86: 11–17

From the writer of this psalm, we have a clear description of what happens when people do not have regard for God. We find in verse 14 the expression ***they have no regard for you***, referring to God. Briefly the following characterize such people:

a. They are arrogant, verse 14;

b. They are ruthless, verse 14. Because they are not like this psalmist, these people who have no regard for God have features opposite to the psalmist's and so:

c. They do not rely on God's faithfulness, verse 11;

d. They do not fear or have reverence for God's name, verse 11;

e. They cannot glorify God's name at any time, verse 12;

f. They do not recognize and will not testify of God's goodness in their lives, verse 13. They are not like the psalmist, and so cannot emulate God and the way He deals with His people specifically, and humankind in general. Because of this situation:

g. They are not compassionate or gracious to people, verse 15;

h. They are quick to anger, lacking in love and fidelity, verse 15;

i.   They are merciless, verse 15. This lack of mercy fuels their ruthless acts, verse 14.

When the characteristics and activities of those who have no regard for God are presented as above, do you now find and accept that there are many people in this class – and they may not even realize that they belong there? When you consider (d) for example i.e. having no reverence for God's Name, is it not a very common thing for people to use God's name carelessly and casually? It is so bad that some Christians do not see anything wrong with it, and don't caution their children; adults and children find it to be in vogue. In the same verse 11, we read that such people do not rely on God's faithfulness; they just cannot trust it, so they have to help themselves 'make it in life.' As you can see, they do not have to be *monsters*, and could well be just like you and me.

CHAPTER 66

Can Glorious Things Be Said of You?

Psalm 87: 1–7

Anything that is shameful is inglorious. For glorious things to be said, the object of such sayings must be wonderful, magnificent and needs to be celebrated. The Bible says very heart-warming things about Jerusalem and the house of God, the temple. Of Jerusalem, we read in Psalm 48:2 that it is the city of the great King. Jerusalem is mentioned hundreds of times in the Bible, spanning the Old Testament and New Testament. God simply chose it to be the city around which numerous things in His calendar of events should revolve. Glorious things are, indeed, documented about this city of God. Verse 5 even suggests that people who are born, or were born, in this city of God would be considered privileged people.

What about you and I who, as Christians, are referred to as the temple of God? – 1 Corinthians 3:16. Take note that Jerusalem, even in its spiritual loftiness, ought to be 'grateful' to be the city that hosted the temple of God. How do you treat your person? What is your relevance as a Christian, if you are one – and wouldn't you seriously consider the glorious things God wants to do in your life and through you, if you desire to become a Christian?

You and I should allow the Highest God Himself be the One to establish us. He is willing and able to establish you in spirit, soul and body. He is able to make you and me to become praise in the earth – the part of the world where you find yourself in. Just like people can say *'this one was born in Zion'*, verse 4, they should be able to say of you and me "This one is *'born of God and knows God'*" – 1 John 4:7.

CHAPTER 67

Who Is Like You, Lord
God Almighty?

Psalm 89: 1–8

This is one of the most marvelous psalms. It is one of the many psalms that extol God. But how do you 'lift up' or exalt him who is higher than the highest of heavens? Psalm 57:5. What we understand is God being higher than the earth. But then we know of children who speak of great things about their parents – in their hearts they hold their parents in high esteem, but they may really not understand the level of their greatness; being human, they may even over-estimate their parents but this option is not possible for us to do towards God.

In this psalm the word 'faithfulness' appears four times.' We find it in verses 1, 2, 5 and 8. Among humankind, faithfulness is uncommon, though God expects it from us. The Word of God tells us that everyone claims to be good or to have unfailing love (and I guess, even the bad people too) but who really can find a faithful person? – Proverbs 20:6. *God is incomparable in faithfulness*. In verse 1, God is faithful in maintaining love forever – this is very difficult, even among many married people. Verse 2 tells us that this faithfulness is established in heaven, and in verse 3 it extends to human beings, using King David as an example – God's faithfulness is the basis of His covenant with David. Verse 5 declares that the holy angels are witnesses of God's faithfulness. From verse 8 we are made to imagine our great God being 'wrapped around' in faithfulness. This makes faithfulness an identity – or a form of identification – for God.

The description of God is completely beyond our natural inclination and ability. None of the heavenly beings can be compared with God – verse 6. He is awesome. But does the fact that we cannot be like God mean that God does not desire that we, His children, should have a resemblance to Him? Which human parent is not glad when told how similar the son or daughter is to them physically, in intelligence, height, mannerism, etc.? Why then do we have such great difficulty in being faithful? At least, our being dependable is feasible.

CHAPTER 68

Unfailing Covenant with The Anointed

Psalm 89: 19–29

Ours is a covenant-keeping God. In King David He exemplified His faithfulness. Although none of us may be able to claim the Davidic Covenant in totality, its contents are worth studying and understanding. The covenant that God has with every Christian is awesome and if only we knew, we would rejoice and make sure that we stay within the confines of the covenant.

A covenant is an agreement between two parties. It is akin to a contract and every contract has its terms clearly embedded or outlined in the body of that contract – unless it is a wishy-washy document crafted by a careless legal practitioner and accepted by concerned parties who are not well-versed in the legal implications of contracts.

In the case of God, He is the one who initiates and maintains the covenants He makes, e.g. the covenant with David. We read that God decided to 'find' David (verse 20), though he was just a young man – for, even in his family, there were older brothers but God chose this younger person and went further to anoint him – verses 19 and 20. Between verses 21 and 29 we find the following parts that God promised to play in his life: sustain and strengthen him; withstand David's enemies and defeat them; exalt David by God's name and make him be above all the kings of the earth; give him influence beyond the rivers and seas; appoint David to be His 'firstborn' – i.e. to hold a pre-eminent position in God's plans; establish His love and maintain David's kingdom forever. Imagine God's part, compared with David's.

What was David's part? To make the LORD his Father, God, Rock and Savior, verse 26.

CHAPTER 69

Covenant: With Discipline and Truth

Psalm 89: 30–37

Every Christian who indeed names the name of Christ, and by His grace is living according to His precepts, must put in enough effort to ensure that they leave a legacy that can be enjoyed by their children and future generations. It is not enough to leave lands and funds for them – a godly and Christian inheritance is very important. But no matter what you do, you will discover that each person in each generation will make decisions and take actions regarding spiritual matters and relationship with God.

The covenant God made was with David but had an extension to his descendants, the greatest Descendant being the Christ, for Jesus also went by the name '**Son of David**' – Matthew 1:1, John 7:42, Mark 10:48, etc. But should the fact that there is a covenant leave one party to the covenant to be serious enough to carry the entire weight of the terms of executing the covenant? And, should the other party be carefree, seemingly oblivious of the demands of the covenant? It does not work that way. God made provision in His contract with David that upon David's decease his descendants could use their free will to act in accordance with the terms of the covenant or go against them. God, therefore, said that there would be disciplinary consequences, verses 30–32. God would independently be true to His covenant, verses 33–36. In verse 37 God ended this theme by using the metaphor of the faithfulness of the moon to show that even in the *'night' of David's descendants' indiscipline*, **God's truth** would still shine and provide *light* for the Covenant. Amen!

CHAPTER 70

The Eternal Versus the Ephemeral

Psalm 90: 1–6, 12

The 'eternal' is God at the pinnacle, and we have angelic creatures who dwell in eternity with God. Humankind, on the other hand, is 'ephemeral' because life on this earth is transient and is limited by time. If you spend some moments to read the passage from which this title is culled, you will find a great and sobering comparison between the eternal and the ephemeral. I encourage you to pick up your Bible and read before you leave this particular chapter for another.

Fortunately, or unfortunately, human beings, like you and I, are both temporal and eternal. During our sojourn on earth, we are ephemeral but after we die, we assume the quality or state of the eternal. This passage, having explained some truths about the eternal and ephemeral pleads with God in verse 12 to *'Teach us to number our days, that we may gain a heart of wisdom.'* But why would we need to apply our hearts to wisdom when willy-nilly we will live on earth, transit from the earth and eventually translate into eternity? I believe it is because on our own we do not, and perhaps cannot, understand the importance of placing this matter in the correct perspective. If God who dwells in eternity does not teach us (or rather if we do not listen or do not believe what He tells us in His Word) we could be making very serious mistakes with eternal consequences. In our present world human beings hardly attain the age of 120 years – and certainly do not reach the age recorded for Noah or Methuselah in the Bible. But how long is eternity? The answer is that eternity is 'endlessness' or eternity may be conceived in terms of infinity. Let us consider this question: If you were asked to make decisions regarding either just tomorrow or the rest of your life, which option would you take? Anyone who really understands the question will choose 'the rest of your life' because you see 'tomorrow' as just another 24 hours that will soon pass. So, how do you take the question of eternity when compared with your time on earth? Which one has more significance – that is if you believe in eternity, for many don't?

CHAPTER 71

Our God Protects His Children

Psalm 91:1–6, 14

Indeed, our God protects His children. It would be counter to nature as we know it for God not to take care of His nature. It is God who created all things and we know that in nature, parents tend to protect their offspring. This is very evident among animals – even wild animals; though a few carnivorous animals are known to devour the young of their kind. But generally, the norm is for God's creatures to seek for the welfare and protection of their young. It is a natural instinct that seems to make them even take risks to self or willingly subject themselves to deprivations to satisfy the survival needs of their young ones. If their young do not 'make it', especially in the wild, the blood-line will not be maintained or perpetuated. The lineage is important, otherwise an entire species could become extinct.

People who subject their lives and way of living to God have Him as their Father. He has made certain promises in the Bible and this passage records one of them; in verse 14 we read *"Because he loves me," says the* Lord, *"I will rescue him; I will protect him, for he acknowledges my name."* This verse is written as God is the One speaking. The benefits recorded in the preceding verses are predicated on a child of God 'acknowledging my (His) name.'

A person who is irreligious, religious but not a Christian, or even a Christian who keeps God at a distance, detaching God from their daily affairs, is not acknowledging His name. You may ask, 'But don't such people make significant and obvious progress in life?' The answer is a big, 'Yes' – they do. They do, because God shows a general goodness to everyone, but His children have the benefits you will find when you read this chapter in its entirety.

CHAPTER 72

Praise and Living Right: Keys to Successful Life

Psalm 92:1–3, 10, 12–15

We know that there are many types of keys. We also know that a key that can open all doors in a big building is both an asset and a liability, depending on who is in custody of, or has access to, it. The commoner situation is for a person to use a key to access a particular door lock. If that key does what it is expected to do and does not have a fault, or the lock does not have a fault, it is well.

This passage tells us of keys to living the Christian life successfully. The keys, as already stated, are praise and living right. Starting with praise, the beginning of this passage tells us that it is a good thing to praise *God for who He is*, verse 1. Even if you do not know the reason for it, just praise God, rather than being grumpy part of, or the entire, day. The psalmist gave a few reasons for his stance on praising God when he mentioned His love and faithfulness, verse 2. With respect to living right, another word for it is righteousness. The words righteousness and holiness sound scary to some readers but it needs not be so. Righteousness simply means living a life that is right and approved by God though it may not be approved by certain people we know, no matter how popular they are in various segments of the society. Clearly, this chapter is not on holiness, but it may be helpful to state here that holiness refers to dedication, reserving oneself and one's affairs for God. It is true that *'The righteous will flourish like a palm tree; they will grow like a cedar of Lebanon'*, verse 12.

The successful Christian life may not necessarily be what the average person who does not yet have proper dealings with God may accept as successful life. If you take John the Baptist as an example, would his fit into the present-day mold of a successful life? Even Jesus Christ Who said that the Son of Man had nowhere to lay His head – would he be regarded as successful in our world today? But they lived successfully for God, doing His will. Every Christian should learn to praise God for Who He is and also live rightly in God's sight.

CHAPTER 73

The Decoration of God's House

Psalm 93:1–5

Decoration is an adornment or ornament that a person applies or wears to show or enhance beauty. Among human beings, even the beautiful or handsome use adornment to look more beautiful or more handsome. But with God would that be the purpose? He is totally wholesome and desirable. So, in the case of God wouldn't it be reasonable to say that anything that goes for adornment is part and parcel of Who He is? And would it not be something that enables us to appreciate His real self though we cannot see God with our naked eyes? 'Seeing' in this case is 'to understand' and create a good mental or spiritual picture or image of the nature or character of God.

In human practice, application of adornment is something external and so, is a decoration on the body or in our immediate environment, like the home, office, car, etc. Adornment may not reflect the true character of a person. This passage describes God's personal adornment for it says that He is robed in, or wears, majesty and strength. The Lord also takes holiness so seriously that apart from being an integral part of His character, holiness adorns (His) house for endless days. This simply means that God cannot tolerate un-holiness. This explains why nobody should expect God to dwell in them in spite of the fact that they are not interested in holiness. 1

Corinthians 6: 19 states that the Christian's body is the temple of the Holy Spirit – God's House. God lives in us through the Holy Spirit, to direct our activities. Among human beings we know that many women like it when their kitchen is clean and orderly. Even when everything is available for cooking and the kitchen has ample space, as long as it is filthy, they will either not be able to use the place or will feel very uncomfortable in such an untidy place. We can extend this to God and conclude that to get the maximum benefits from God every Christian must take holiness as one of our priorities especially when we remember what Jesus Christ said, that we must abide in Him as without Him we cannot achieve anything positive (John 15: 4).

CHAPTER 74

Behavior of the Wicked

Psalm 94: 1–11

It is not difficult to know who a person is, even though many people tend to hide their true, bad, character. But the character of a person is eventually revealed by the things the person says, approves of or does openly. That little bit that is open to the public (in this case anyone other than the person concerned) is enough for one who is very sensitive or analytical to make a correct judgment about the real person.

In the Bible we read in Proverbs 20: 11 that it is possible and easy to know the kind of person a child is. And in most instances the traits and behaviors demonstrated in childhood grow as the person increases in age; this means that people will continue seeing the good qualities or the bad qualities as they are more and more evident. It is God Who can stop the bad or terrible qualities from growing. This is because Satan, the enemy of humankind, does not wish the person with a bad trait well or the society well.

This passage tells us of the behavior of wicked people. It tells us the following: They rejoice or find great pleasure and joy in doing evil; they speak with arrogance and are full of boasting; they are not interested in those who are in dire need e.g. widows, strangers and orphans, and do not even mind killing them or doing things that could cause their death. The

Word of God calls these people foolish, because wickedness and foolishness go together. Wicked people behave the way they do partly because they feel that there is no God – and even when they believe there is God their behavior shows that they do not think God will call them to account for their bad behavior.

CHAPTER 75

The Fruit of Stubbornness

Psalm 95:1–11

Stubbornness is seen in human beings of all ages, be they children or adults. This insistence on doing what one wants to do can be very irritating to parents and teachers in the early stages of the education of a child. In children stubbornness frequently leads them to make mistakes that could have been avoided because the older people who guide children aimed at preventing the mistakes from happening. When a child learns from the negative consequences of stubbornness, it is a good thing. Unfortunately, many children grow into adulthood and carry along stubbornness even till old age.

It is not every time that stubbornness is bad; if the stubbornness is based on proven facts that are available to the stubborn person, while other people do not have such information, the person may proceed to carry out the intended plan and the results will prove such a person right. From the foregoing it is clear that stubbornness, though it is frequently a bad thing, may be a good thing in certain cases.

However, when it is a matter between a person and God, stubbornness towards the declared will of God as found in the Bible is almost always followed by bad and painful results; sometimes it may have negative eternal results.

The passage used for this chapter shows that the ancient Israelites hardened their hearts against God Who was good to them and they refused to have a fixed heart and attitude towards Him; rather their minds strayed to foreign gods and their appetite or desire for what they wanted when they wanted had no end. God was unhappy with them for forty years and most of them did not enter the Promised Land. God will satisfy our needs but we may have to endure some pain.

CHAPTER 76

Joy Is for All Creation

Psalm 96:1–13

Psalm 96 takes us beyond the common thinking or belief that praise to God is expected only from humankind. In this passage we find that the Psalmist went further to tell us that we should know that not only we the human beings praise God. This is a very important piece of fact because we know that in many societies, praises are heaped on people. This does not mean that praising people who do well is wrong.

It is a good thing to praise human beings as we find that even young children recognize and appreciate the praises that are given to them by parents and family members when they achieve or exceed expectations – and parents should not shy away from doing that for their children. At school, pupils and students rejoice when they are commended for stellar performances in academics, sports, leadership, etc. Adults of all ages do not fail to display various awards at work and at both the community and national levels. When praise is not recognized or withheld, people who deserve it are not pleased and may actually be discouraged or de-motivated.

You will discover from verses 11–13 that as you are whining about your current or past situation (and maybe also your apparent foggy future), God's entire non-human creation is busy praising God, leaving you out of the picture. The verses show that the heavens, the seas, the fields, the forests – and *everything* that can be found in them *'rejoice before the Lord'*. They praise God in their own way.

This certainly brings to remembrance what Jesus Christ, in Luke 19: 40, told the Jewish leaders who complained about the Hallelujah piled on Him during His Triumphal entry: that even stones would cry out or burst into cheers if humans were prevented from doing so. It is wonderful to play your role in praises to God.

CHAPTER 77

Joy: For the Oceans, Mountains and Me

Psalm 98:4–9

It should be evident that Joy precedes Praise. Many of the Psalms show this fact. A person who is in a somber mood has a very high mountain to climb to be able to praise God. This does not mean that the person who is not happy cannot praise God. Some people believe, and correctly so, that happiness depends on happenings, but joy depends on Jesus. What this means is that there may be joy inside the life of a person though there may be troubles happening around (or even surrounding) the person's life.

The above may sound contradictory, but it is the experience of many Christians who know and choose to practice this truth as a way of life; it did not start today, and we have good examples in Paul and Silas, for it is recorded in Acts 16: 25 that *'About midnight Paul and Silas were praying and singing hymns to God, and the other prisoners were listening to them.'* Jail is not a normal or natural place to praise God, unless some Christian group is on a visit, and the members are the ones conducting a service for the inmates. But here, the joy that was 'in the inside' of these prisoners prompted them to create a session of praise in spite of their adversity. They proved to us that it is possible to praise God in adverse circumstances.

It is only possible to *'Shout for joy to the Lord, all the earth, burst into jubilant song with music'* as Psalm 98: 4 admonishes us if, and only if, we *look beyond and above* our discomfort, unfavorable financial status, poor health condition, uncertain employment, etc. and look up to and 'see' God, through our Lord Jesus Christ, in such unwelcome circumstances.

Finally, we shall learn from the sea, rivers, and mountains. *The sea:* "Let the sea resound, and everything in it," verse 7. *The rivers:* "Let the rivers clap their hands", verse 8. *The mountains:* "Let the mountains sing together for joy", verse 8. All these, you and I, are to sing before the Lord, verse 9. It is a wonderful thing for the non-human creatures of God to join hands with us to praise God out of the joy we all experience.

CHAPTER 78

Serving the Lord with Gladness

Psalm 100:1–5

It cannot be gainsaid that irrespective of the fact that many workers love their work, there are a sizeable number of employees who do not meet the demands of their work, principally because they are not happy with the work.

Attitude and training have a lot to do with a positive and satisfying response to work. Work when taken as service, could help the grumbling worker. When you know that you are rendering service you clearly understand that you are not working for the sake of working. The person who benefits from your service could actually be you. A student's negative attitude towards school work may change dramatically when the discomfort of daily and progressively challenging academic work is recognized as an essential precursor to having a satisfying future – in future it will be clear that all the service was primarily for yourself.

Verse 2 of this passage tells us to *'Worship the LORD with gladness.'* Indeed, Worship is a spiritual work that Christians perform to God; it makes sense and is beneficial to us and is acceptable to God only if we carry out this service with gladness. God deserves our worship.

CHAPTER 79

In Times of Loneliness, Fear and Tears

Psalm 102:1–7,9,17

When in times of loneliness, fear and tears this psalmist stated in verse 17: *'He will respond to the prayer of the destitute; he will not despise their plea.'* The truth regarding you and me is that we really do not fancy times of loneliness, fear and tears.

Unfortunately, as long as we are alive anywhere in this world, we will have at least one incident of loneliness, fear and tears. Some of them are self-inflicted due to the unguided or even stubborn decisions we make; at other times these periods of life occur no matter what we do. The earlier we know that even godly children, youth, men and women are not immune to the reverses of life the better for us.

It will be very illuminating for you to read the above passage in your Bible to appreciate the variety and degree of challenges that this psalmist faced. He was a man of God but he went through unfortunate conditions that affected his body, appetite, mind, sleep and relationships.

We must know that when people notice that things are not well with us, the natural thing is for many of them to abandon us, leaving us *'like a bird alone on a roof'* – verse 7; this happens even when the people are close to us – like family members, friends and colleagues. But when we have this experience, do we or will we always know what to do? The answer is to do like this psalmist – make a fervent plea to God with the full assurance that He will listen and see you through it.

CHAPTER 80

Our God: Forgiving, Redeeming, Providing

Psalm 103:1–8,13

Frank forgetfulness, neglecting to remember and behaving like an issue has been forgotten are all maladies of human beings. Some people who say they have forgotten something may actually choose what to forget and what not to forget – a form of selective forgetfulness.

It is, therefore, possible for a person to remember all the bad things and forget all the good things. Those who remember all the bad things that have happened to them, especially the ones that people did to them (or they conclude that people did to them) may have difficulty with forgiving. People who forget all the good things that have happened to them, including all the good things that people brought their way, are certainly ingrates.

In many ways, however, a balanced memory of both good and nasty experiences can help us make progress and mature in every area of our lives. In verse 2 of this passage we read: *'and forget not all his benefits.'* God has given us many benefits and there is a tendency to forget them or even take them for granted. When you look through the short list you discover that the benefits include things like forgiveness, healing, redemption, youthfulness and provision of good things generally. His mercy, compassion and patience are all things that many of us see as our rights. Indeed, our God forgives, redeems, and continues to provide for humankind.

CHAPTER 81

Wisdom and Purpose in God's Creation

Psalm 104:10–14,18–24

Close observation of God's creation reveals that there are both wisdom and purpose in even the minute things that He made. Nothing seems to have been left to chance. Is it at the level of micro-organisms like bacteria, fungi, viruses, etc. or the level of the visible creatures like trees and animals, or yet, the heavenly bodies and expanding space? In all of these, there is a purpose, even where humankind has yet not been able to identify all that is in God's cosmos or the purpose in them.

The psalmist penned a nice summary using the landscape of his time as he described the mountains, valleys, the animals therein, etc. He tells us that night and day have their purposes. Some animals prey at night, and sleep in the daylight hours; we, at the apex of God's creation, generally sleep and night, and work in the daytime. Of course, we know that our desire to work and achieve significant prosperity in a lifetime has pushed man to break the boundaries and work round-the-clock, with or without shift duty.

He did not fail to tell us the purpose of sunshine, rainfall and the various seasons. None of these have failed to perform their duties and science has proved that our survival depends on the predictable characteristic of 'nature'. Though he limited himself to the earth the psalmist ended this passage by stating: *'In wisdom you made them all; the earth is full of your creatures.'*

CHAPTER 82

From Few to Many; From Prisoner to Governor

Psalm 105:1, 12–22

Isn't it a thing of wonder to consider the kind of things that God does for His people in particular and for humankind in general? The title: *From Few to Many; From Prisoner to Governor* is very apt for the story of the ancient Israelites using one of them, Joseph, as a special example.

Till today many people wonder why the people of Israel should be considered the chosen of God – and some people actually take serious offense over that status. Indeed, the Bible has stated that the Israelites were not necessarily the best of people to be known as God's special people – various passages e.g. Jeremiah 7: 25, 26 and Acts 7:51, 52 show that they were stiff-necked, insisted on having their way and resisted God almost continuously. God still decided to choose them, and there is nothing anyone can do about it, as human beings cannot castigate or query God.

They started off as Abraham's family and are now an entire nation influencing many things on earth. Truly God rebuked and punished even kings and various peoples on their behalf and did the miracle of a stranger becoming a governor of Egypt. Such are the ways of God and He has not changed. God's mercy and grace are still the vehicles that God uses to bless people – even people from insignificant backgrounds. He has a way of elevating individuals and groups of people.

CHAPTER 83

Confessing, Yet Forgetting?

Psalm 106:1–15

Confession is essential in normal human relationships. In many things we offend people, see James 3:2, and confession is necessary to heal wounds in parent-child, marital, workplace and church relationships. The Old and New Testaments have a number of examples of confessions.

In the New Testament the apostle James urged the early Christians to confess when he said: *"Therefore confess your sins to each other and pray for each other so that you may be healed"* – James 5:16. When people make confession what is expected is that the confession comes from conviction, sorrow and a desire not to perpetuate or repeat the sin or fault. Without these ingredients, confession tends to be an act to *fulfil all righteousness*.

When it is between two people like husband and wife, brother and sister, two colleagues, etc. confession is easier than when more people are involved; in the latter case they all must accept that a wrong has been done or a sin has been committed. Most people-groups are not willing to do that as some will argue against accepting a fault, especially when lawyers are involved.

It is, therefore, interesting that in this psalm an entire community was involved in confession as we read in verse 6: *"We have sinned, even as our ancestors did; we have done wrong and acted wickedly."* This is commendable. In this case they confessed to God. Proper confession, forgetting the subject of confession, and God's mercy do not go together; the combination only leads to repeated acts, and repeated confessions. Is that not what happens to many of us? We need a change and not be like the ancient Israelites who, after confessions, *"soon forgot what he had done and did not wait for his plan to unfold"* – verse 13.

CHAPTER 84

Envy with Idolatry

Psalm 106:16–27

Numbers 16 tells this unparalleled story of envy and rebellion. Three leaders, one from the tribe of Levi (Korah) and two – the ones referred to in this psalm – from the tribe of Reuben (Dathan and Abiram) instigated this rebellion. Every reader will agree that envy is rife in our world, and sometimes it is considered an acceptable vice in families, workplaces, professions, and businesses.

Since there is limited space, we shall concentrate on two things that envy does to the envious: (a) It does not allow them to 'see' goodness in themselves or their situation; in this story about ancient Israelites *"…. they despised the **pleasant** land; they did not believe his promise"*, verse 24. (b) Envy makes people see faults in virtually everything around them and destroys gratitude. Still referring to the Israelites we read in verse 25 *"They grumbled in their tents and did not obey the LORD."* They rather envied Moses and Aaron.

However, when it comes to idolatry, many modern, intellectual, readers will not agree that it is in practice today. In verse 20 this psalm indicates that Israel *"…exchanged their glorious God for an image of a bull,"* We therefore find that anytime anybody worships or reveres *anything* rather than, or above God, that is idolatry in practice. That may well be an object, principle, practice or personality – visible or invisible. You may fill in the gaps and figure idolatry out.

This psalm also tells us two things that idolatry does viz.: a) it demands worship, verse 19; b) it makes people forget, for we read in verse 21 that the Israelites at the time *"…forgot the God who saved them,"* You and I must therefore be on the watch-out that we do not create anything or allow anything in our lives that can make us forget God or relegate Him to the background.

CHAPTER 85

Intervening

Psalm 106:28–33

Phinehas is not one of the well-known characters of the Old Testament. His name appears in the genealogy of the Levites in Exodus 6:25 as the grandson of Aaron, and in Numbers 25 in what we today would consider a gruesome act vis-à-vis the causative series of events.

The death of any individual or groups of people gives us concern. The account is sobering and the opinion one holds depends on the eyes with which it is viewed – yours and mine or God's. This story on intervention and explanatory note are included because many people who are familiar with the story hold negative opinion about this very incident.

From the eyes of God idolatry is seen as an affront to God because He says we should revere Him – Exodus 20:3; He also desires that we honor/respect ourselves as human beings whom He has set at the zenith of creation – Psalm 8:5. When idolatry is mixed with sexual immorality – which is the situation referred to in this passage (with details in Numbers 25) – it is odious to God, and He is highly offended, perhaps because of the spiritual connotations. With ancient Israel, there was no longer any distinction between them and the nations round about them.

Various sexual practices abound today and many societies have given citizens the right to do what they want, today; unfortunately, God is not swayed in their majority direction, and still stands by His original plan. You may refer to 1 Corinthians 6:12-20 and in particular verse 18. If a good percentage of people consider homosexuality simply an orientation, or the way a person was born, you can imagine the general attitude towards fornication and adultery. Numbers 25 indicates that 24,000 died in one day and Phinehas' intervention terminated the ongoing scourge. In the face of looming or current catastrophic global, national, or regional concerns, the appropriate leaders and organizations would be seen as shirking their responsibility of saving lives if they stay quiet, doing nothing, simply because they do not want to ruffle feathers of the populace; they act principally because it is morally right to save lives even when discomfort is the price that people have to pay. In our families, etc. we must intervene as soon as things go wrong and avoid drastic steps like Phinehas'. If you and I intervene in a timely manner, issues are nipped in the bud.

CHAPTER 86

Conformity Is Costly

Psalm 106:34–48

Conformity is the one of the easiest options to adopt when faced with difficult situations, especially issues of survival. Survival and 'moving forward' may be what children and young people have to do in the boarding house to pass examination; survival and 'moving forward' may well be strategies applied to one's career or business. Conformity is a challenge that we face, have faced or will face – it is a matter of time. But how should we handle it?

The Israelites in the time preceding the psalmist's documentation of the facts in this chapter received specific instructions from God and they had to weigh the consequences of being the 'peculiar people' God desired in Exodus 19:5 *"Now if you obey me fully and keep my covenant, then out of all nations you will be my treasured possession."* They decided against this special status the way many people are still doing today. What they preferred was the easier job in that *"…they mingled with the nations and adopted their customs."* Even as you read this, it remains easier to mingle or conform than to stand out for the Lord.

This passage tells us the consequences of conformity as including: idolatry, human sacrifice, desecration of land (and all landed property), self-defilement, subjugation, and ruin by sin. None of the listed effects of conformity is cheap – all of them are costly.

The consequences of conformity are frequently long-lasting and could be eternal. The problems are the ease of conformity and the sheer number of conformists. It is not easy to determinedly follow God and His ways – but doing so paves the way for a good future for every bold doer.

CHAPTER 87

Let the Redeemed Say So

Psalm 107:1–16

A redeemer pays a price to free somebody from indebtedness, or the bad effects of certain decisions or actions taken. In the Bible, the Redeemer is Jesus Christ, and He paid the ultimate price to atone for, or expiate, the sin of humankind. Individuals frequently find themselves needing redemption in normal daily activities; this is because wrong decisions are made, just as wrong transactions are undertaken.

We read from verse 2: *"Let the redeemed of the LORD tell their story –"* as part of the experiences of Israelites of old. Four action words show the need for redemption in the experiences of these people – the words are: *wandered*, verse 4; *suffering*, verse 10; *rebelled*, verse 11, and *stumbled*, verse 12.

From the passage, we find four situational words indicating their condition – the words are: *wastelands*, verse 4; *trouble* and *distress*, verse 6; *darkness*, verses 10 and 14 and repeat of *distress*, verse 13. The link is that the *actions* produced the sad *situations,* necessitating *redemption*. It still happens.

The story of the redeemed is best told by the redeemed. Testimonies make most sense when given by those who have been impacted directly. The redeemed have the duty of telling their testimonies, because what their testimonies do for their hearers is two-fold viz.: *warning* and *encouragement.* The warning is that listeners should refrain from walking the same paths as the testifier; the encouragement is from the fact that God has actually done these things for someone like them.

Indeed, let the redeemed of the Lord say so. *"Let them give thanks to the LORD for his unfailing love and his wonderful deeds…"* verse 15.

CHAPTER 88

I Will Awaken the Dawn

Psalm 108:1–9

When we go to bed, not everyone wakes up the next day. Of the people that wake up, a poll will prove that not everyone is happy. How will all and sundry be happy when some wake up in pain, in debt, in frustration, in anger, in confusion, in physical or spiritual jail, without hope or help, etc.? They are not ungrateful that they are awake, but they have a relatively clear idea how the day will proceed once again and how it will eventually end.

The above do not totally describe the situations that some people grapple with. Some people feel that they should knock themselves out of reality with drugs or alcohol – and they do it. Many refuse to get out of bed until long after waking up; the day seems to drag its feet, and everything and everybody seems to contribute to their distress. The above feeling has happened to virtually everybody at one time or the other – but for many it seems to be the order of the day.

You will notice that this psalmist in the first two verses penned the words: *"My heart, O God, is steadfast; I will sing and make music with all my soul. Awake, harp and lyre. I will awaken the dawn."* The title of this write-up is taken from verse 2, *"I will awaken the dawn."* He did not say that the dawn would awaken him but vice-versa.

Something must be in the mind of a person who is awake before the dawn 'wakes up' – and that thing must be important. Ask a young couple preparing for the activities of their wedding; a student preparing for a final-year examination; a young employee about to assume duty in a good place of work, and all of them will tell you they virtually awoke the dawn. This psalmist awakened the dawn to praise the Lord. Will you and I follow in his steps and get excited to praise the Lord early in the day?

CHAPTER 89

Spiritual Boomerang

Psalm 109:1–20

The ricochet or bounce-back we find in life can take different forms – frightening, entertaining, satisfying, humbling, etc. This bounce-back effect spares no area of life, showing that we all have to be careful to do the right or avoid doing the wrong. Doing the right surely has its rebound, and same goes for wrongdoing. Spiritual life is not excluded – and indeed cannot be excluded – as physical, social, academic, political actions and decisions have spiritual undertones that we may either be aware of or unaware of.

If you read the psalm you will find that the activities and events were really day-to-day issues that did not seem to matter to the people concerned, especially the perpetrators. They did not care a hoot about the effects that their utterances or actions had on people. In verses 3 and 4 we read: *"… they attack me without cause. In return for my friendship they accuse me, …."* Verse 5 records: *"They repay me evil for good, and hatred for my friendship."* From verses 6 to 15 we see curses that emanate from bitterness of heart consequent upon these evil actions on the psalmist, and other evil acts carried out against people as recorded from verses 16 to 18, which are actually given as solid reasons for these strong sentiments and prayers.

Indeed, you must be familiar with Apostle Paul's admonition in Romans 12:14 *'Bless those who persecute you, bless and do not curse'*; similarly, our Lord Jesus Christ told us in Luke 6:28 *'bless those who curse you, pray for those who mistreat you.'* The essence of these instructions is for us to show the vile person mercy, *'Be merciful, just as your Father is merciful'* – Luke 6:36. Showing the merciless mercy is providing them with a long rope to repent and change their ways. However, should they persist in such unwholesome ways, the spiritual boomerang will eventually take place. We should be interested in ensuring that what we do will cause only positive rebound for us and our family members.

CHAPTER 90

Melchizedek

Psalm 110:1–10

This passage is one of the messianic psalms, referring primarily to Jesus Christ. Melchizedek was a twin-significant personality; this is because he was both king and priest – Genesis 14:18. A king used to rule over people and have absolute authority and power – and they still do in certain parts of the world, with some modification in other places. A priest in the Old Testament represented God on earth in spiritual matters and he was an intermediary between God and human beings. The Bible refers to Melchizedek as both king of Salem and priest of the Highest God as we find in Hebrews 7 and Genesis 14. Melchizedek's priesthood preceded the priesthood of Aaron and, incidentally, he was the only human being who occupied this priesthood.

A similarly unique office was later occupied by the Lord Jesus Christ and that is why His priesthood is referred to as 'after the Order of Melchizedek', Hebrews 5:6-10 and 6:20. Jesus Christ, the Son of God, humbled Himself and actually suffered in obedience to the will of God, Hebrews 5:8. The Bible does not have record of any person who fits this peculiar twin-office. There is nobody who has successfully claimed to be King of Kings, Lord of Lords and also Priest of the Highest. Nobody can replicate what Jesus Christ did because the sacrifice He made was the sacrifice of Himself and is the zenith of all sacrifices. Like in the case of Melchizedek, Jesus has no successor – His priesthood started and ended with Him.

We find these two special characters in the Bible – Melchizedek and Jesus Christ. Jesus is, however, superior in spite of the similarity; this is because He is more than just king of Salem and verse 2 of this passage says his business is to *"Rule in the midst of your enemies!"* and we know that in future *"he will crush kings on the day of his wrath"* – verse 5. Having Jesus as your friendly King is worth more than anything you can think of.

CHAPTER 91

Beginning of Wisdom

Psalm 111:1–10

The beginning of anything is its starting point or foundation. The Book of Proverbs tells us that wisdom is the principal thing, Proverbs 4:7 *KJV*. It also tells us that the knowledge of the Holy One is understanding, Proverbs 9:10. Verse 10 of our Psalms passage tells us: "The fear of the Lord is the beginning of wisdom…" When juxtaposed, these verses seem to tell us that: 'The fear of the LORD is the beginning of the principal thing' in life.

We are aware of people who really did not care about God yet they appeared (and the contemporary ones appear) to be wise and successful. If there are such people who are comfortable with relegating God to the background and various segments of the society recognize and respect them, do the contents of these verses not appear contradictory? I would say, no; and what of you? To my mind, the experiences of such men and women do not contradict the Word of God in any way because what people usually see is the surface. God sees the hearts of people and He knows that whoever does not have fear (awe, reverence, respect or regard) for God misses a lot – both in life and hereafter. What would the lives of such people be *if* they had the knowledge of the Holy One (God) in addition to what the Holy One put into them? Wouldn't they have been more prominent and wouldn't they have contributed more to their families and societies? The first and second parts of verse 10 actually state: "The fear of the Lord is the beginning of wisdom; all who follow his precepts have good understanding." Indeed, to the average onlooker, and sometimes to Christians, people who do not live their lives for God still do well but the truth remains that they are not at their best.

CHAPTER 92

On Having A Good Plan for Your Family

Psalm 112:1–10

Every normal person who bears even one child makes arrangements for that child. It is in the character of normal parents to have plans for their children. However, there are parents and *there are parents.* By this statement consideration is given only to those parents who plan well for their children, as there is not enough space here to comment on those who just have families but have no thought about plans for their spouses or their children. Worldwide, all parents who actually plan for their children ensure that they provide at least the basics of food, shelter and clothing. Beyond these three, almost all reasonable parents strongly consider the health and education of their children – even if they did not attain the level of education that they may have desired. Every good parent wants their children to surpass them.

But like stated above, there are yet some parents who are in a special category. In this category are parents who are described in this psalm. They go beyond what every other parent does; they go beyond time and think of eternity for their children; they go beyond the physical and pay close attention to the spiritual. Do you belong to this special group or if you are not yet a parent, do you aspire to, when you become a parent? These parents live out and make their children see and imbibe righteousness, grace, compassion, generosity, justice, etc. Remember that when these parents do the foregoing *'their righteousness endures forever'* – verse 8 and *'the generation of the upright will be blessed'* – verse 6.

We can come to the conclusion that having a good plan for members of our families covers every aspect of life. If we believe what the Bible teaches about human life, we will know that we are here temporarily. We should not worry about our parents that may not have known this will of God about our planning *comprehensively* for our children. We know, and so we should give a prominent place to the spiritual growth, maturity and fulfillment of our children and not just stop at providing the things that will end here.

CHAPTER 93

Praises from Sunrise to Sunset

Psalm 113:1–9

This passage tells us *'Let the name of the Lord be praised, both now and forevermore. From the rising of the sun to the place where it sets, the name of the Lord is to be praised'* – verses 2 and 3. Praises do not just emanate. Agents of praise may be 'beings' or 'objects' i.e. instruments. For the praise timing of *'From the rising of the sun to the place where the sun sets'* the appropriate agents include those that function in the daytime e.g. humans; for '*forevermore*' those are eternal beings like angels and humankind in eternity.

Starting with verse 1 which states: *'Praise the Lord, you his servants; praise the name of the Lord',* we readily find that those that should praise the Lord are *His servants.* But who are His servants? The answer can be obtained partly from verses 2 and 3, and partly from the rest of the psalm. We can extract from these verses that God's servants are the agents that do His will, attend to Him, and obey Him in everything.

We can safely say that *the entire creation functions as God's servants* for the King James Version states in Revelation 4: 11 that God has created all things, and for his pleasure they are, and were created. You will notice that in this psalm the psalmist limited the time frame of his song to the daylight hours; in those hours it is mainly human beings who are naturally awake and active. In conjunction with the multitude of God's creatures that share this time frame for their normal activities, they should praise God. There are many creatures that function in darkness and that is their time to praise their maker.

Psalm 103: 21 tells us of God's servants or ministers who do His pleasure. You may refer to that verse and find out who they are. It should be noted that God sometimes uses people as His servants to accomplish His desires without the people even knowing so – e.g. King Nebuchadnezzar in Jeremiah 25: 9 and King Cyrus in Isaiah 44: 28. It is obvious from this psalm that our God deserves praise both in time and in eternity. Amen!

CHAPTER 94

Enslaved by Idols; Blessed by God

Psalm 115:3–8,13–15

There are instances where people may find themselves in concomitant or consecutive relationships that have opposite consequences. This may be inadvertent, with the person or persons in the center of such relationships not realizing at the beginning what the results would be. It could also be as a result of adventure, e.g. some children, young or even older people attempting things with obvious results but with the funny belief that they would escape bad results, reaping only benefits.

Israelites, in the time of (and, preceding) writing this psalm, decided to deal with both the God of their forefathers and the idols of the peoples of neighboring nations. We thus find Israel in situations of being *enslaved by idols; blessed by God* depending on their choice at any point in time. With regards to idols and idolatry verse 8 says: *'Those who make them will be like them, and so will all who trust in them.'* The earlier verses indicate the alluded similarity in worthlessness and non-functionality. Guilty Israelites, just like the neighbors they copied, knew that these physical, man-made idols had various body parts but they did not do what they usually do. This truth did not deter them, as they went headlong into idolatry. What good did they expect to come out of this ill-advised adventure?

In Jeremiah 5:25 and 12:30 God gave the warning that idols would be a snare, or trap, to His people and so they should beware of them. May we all choose rightly, especially in these days that idols come in various forms – some subtle, and some attractive. Some idols look innocuous and some are very popular – so popular that even experienced Christians may not readily identify them, especially if they are careless.

With God, verses 13–15 indicate a complete opposite of the above thus: '*he will bless those who fear the* LORD*— small and great alike. May the* LORD *cause you to flourish, both you and your children. May you be blessed by the* LORD, *the Maker of heaven and earth.*'

CHAPTER 95

Trusting in Man or God?

Psalm 118:8,9,14,17,21–24

If you ask an average person *in your daily activities do you trust in God, people or government?* the quick answer you are very likely to receive is, *God*. If you probe for examples as proof of their assertion, you should not be surprised, especially if the person is a Christian, that the reaction will be that of offense at the *affront* by you. How dare you query their trust in God, or how dare you treat them like they are unbelievers in the Lord God?

The truth is that many of us have not sat down to analyze our actions, motives, reactions, interests, etc.? For those who are very religious, go to church and do as many right things as possible – especially when compared with other people that they know or read about – those activities are enough proof that they trust in God. But how many of us would not feel intimidated by Job's statement *Though God slays me, yet will I trust in him* in Job 13: 15? It simply means even if God would cause him to die, he would not doubt God but still trust Him. Trusting in what you see tends to be easier than what you do not see – and certainly easier than *Who* you cannot, and will never see, in your lifetime. This is the reason why it takes faith to trust in God. The interesting thing is that what and who you 'see' may not be as reliable as what you do not see. Faith in itself has to be predicated on what is true and reliable. It, therefore, makes sense that the fact that you have taken visual note of the presence of a chair in the far end of a room or hall does not mean that it is a reliable chair to sit on. Ditto applies to many *princes* and other human beings as stated in verses 8 and 9 of this psalm: *'It is better to take refuge in the* LORD *than to trust in humans. It is better to take refuge in the* LORD *than to trust in princes.'* I believe that you took note of the fact that verse 9 singles out princes to reemphasize that they are not different from the rest of humanity; they may be resplendent in their appearance and ways of doing things, but they are the same as everyone else. It is better to trust in God because God is faithful.

CHAPTER 96

The Challenge of Youth

Psalm 119:9–16

Every stage of life has its own challenge(s). This is true right from life in the womb to old age. The challenge of youth is myriad but the aspect treated by this psalm is Purity. Youth is a very impressionable stage of our lives – being an extension of the adventure and experimentation in life. Experience is limited in this stage of life and it is unfair for significantly more to be expected of youth. The average young person, especially in the early segment of that age bracket, tends to want to blend in with age-mates, both the ones in their immediate environment and those on the far-flung global scene. Youths thus tend to mingle with similarly-aged people at school, residential estate or other neighborhood, club, church, and beyond. They get easily hooked on to the Internet and associate with all manner of youths in the virtual space, whether they are actual youths, feigned 'youths' or confirmed predators of any age.

It is, therefore, more significant in these times to not only broach the topic of purity but also to pay a closer attention to it in detail. But why is purity significant at this stage of life? I believe it is because this is when a firm foundation on this matter is built – positively or negatively. A good firm foundation will stand the test of time; sadly, a firm foundation built on filth will plague the mind, thought, decisions and actions of a youth till old age – unless the Lord is given the chance to intervene.

So, to the question *'How can a young person stay on the path of purity?'* the passage provides appropriate answers viz.: *'living according to your word'*, hiding God's word in the heart, allowing God to be the teacher, meditating or ruminating on the truth, and refusing to neglect it. Finally, each Christian youth must say: *'I rejoice in following your statutes as one rejoices in great riches.'* This can only be said with confidence after appropriating the answers just listed – and it does not matter if you have passed the age of youth.

CHAPTER 97

In Whose Company?

Psalm 119:57–64

The type of people that make up the company of a person determines or indicates who the person really is. This is especially true when the person has options but goes for a particular set of people. The assertion is further strengthened when the person is continually in the gathering of that category of persons.

A person who spends significant time after work in a club house, drinking with *friends,* is either an alcoholic or on an inexorable path towards becoming one. When a young person or an apparently decent older person takes pleasure in hanging out with drug addicts, it could be that the person is tilting towards the vice of drug use and eventual addiction. The same extrapolation can be made of a teenager who is disobedient to parents and chooses to keep company with older girls who are known in the community as commercial sex workers.

On the other hand, a well-known average student who chooses the star of the class as friend will, over time, become a strong student – it is easier for the one with a desire to improve on grades to get better; the excellent student will not drop in grades from deepening their knowledge through teaching a friend.

In spiritual matters, the kind of company a person keeps also determines a lot. If you want to make progress in your Christian life, it is imperative to associate with people of like mind, including those you can look up to. In this passage there are very instructive guidelines: *'Though the wicked bind me with ropes, I will not forget your law',* verse 61 – doggedness and sense of purpose; and *'I am a friend to all who fear you, to all who follow your precepts',* verse 63 – the useful company to keep. For your own good in every facet of life, you must learn to make and maintain the right company. For the reader who is a parent or grandparent, do not be surprised that your children and grandchildren may watch, and emulate your choices in this matter also.

CHAPTER 98

Wisdom from Above

Psalm 119:97–104

The source and type of information we imbibe have profound effect on the quality of knowledge we have. The quality of knowledge we have also determines the degree of wisdom we have, or otherwise. If we take wisdom to mean the application, usually to at least our advantage, of the knowledge we acquire it is evident that wisdom is very paramount in our lives. There is no need to send your son or daughter to a school at any level if the teachers are not well equipped with the information that will make your child grow up to become a wise adult. The passage for this chapter tells us of a very important well of wisdom which is none other than God Himself. Because God is this wonderful resource, we have every justification to trust Him and so we can put into practice whatever is in His Word. God is reliable and the ways of humans are engraved on His palm.

In verse 102 this psalmist said *'I have not departed from your laws, for you yourself have taught me.'* He knew why he should stick to the truth from God, one of the strong reasons being the immense value he obtained from those established foundations of life, for in verses 98–100 he said: *'Your commands are always with me and make me wiser than my enemies. I have more insight than all my teachers, for I meditate on your statutes. I have more understanding than the elders, for I obey your precepts.'* He was not cocky or looking down on his enemies, teachers and elders; we know how unwise some people who have ignored God have lived, missing the point even in their personal, family and spiritual lives. What made the difference between this psalmist and the others was God's commands which he kept with him always. Anybody who does what he did is a wise person, and the stage of life the person is in does not matter. May you be able to, one day, say convincingly like this psalmist: *'How sweet are your words to my taste, sweeter than honey to my mouth!'* – verse 103.

CHAPTER 99

The Faithful Helper and Keeper

Psalm 121:1–8

Synonyms of faithfulness include fidelity, truthfulness, accuracy and authenticity. Every time you read or think of God as the Faithful One it would be good to remember these other words. It is difficult to apply the word *faithfulness* to every human being you come in contact with because some people have the tendency to be deceptive, slippery, inaccurate and unreal. People are unfaithful both in their minds and by their actions. Unless this reader is too young you will corroborate the fact that, at least once so far in your life, you have experienced the shock of disappointment from someone or people you considered reliable and truthful.

We all know that security is very important in our affairs and that is why our airports, roads, homes, schools and offices have been installed with security gadgets. It is for the very reason that you cannot know what is in the heart of a human being that many families prefer dogs to humans as home guards.

God is completely different and what He said He will do, He will do; what He said He stands against, He has not changed His mind about them. Indeed, God is our Help, Guide and Protector. Verses 2 and 3 of this passage say categorically: *My help comes from the LORD, the Maker of heaven and earth. He will not let your foot slip—he who watches over you will not slumber;'* Why are the two keywords – help and watch – so important? At one point or another in our lives we need help and we also need protection. The *help* we need may be advice, support, guidance, etc.; God is able to provide these directly from the Bible, a gentle nudge by the Holy Spirit, or through the agency of people, circumstances, etc. The *protection* we need may be by God directing us away from physical danger, danger from what could come out of our mouths, danger from unwise decisions, and shielding us from physical harm. May we all put our trust in God who is faithful in His nature, word and dealings with us.

CHAPTER 100

Restoration

Psalm 126:1–6

Restoration presupposes something gone awry. Something must have gone wrong or off-track before it needs restoration. The original plan is no longer what the current reality is. In our world, things are today not what God intended at creation. When you re-read the creation account in the early part of Genesis you find that God said that what He did was good, and after creation of humankind He said it was *very good* – Genesis 1:27, 28, 31. We all agree that the state of our world, many countries, communities and individuals is not good. This is why restoration is necessary. Our personal plans sometimes find deviations as we go on in life – and this is not referring to many people who do not know what to do in life and, when they do, they do not plan.

The passage actually refers to Jerusalem; we should know that Jerusalem has seen plenty of trouble and has had a really checkered history. Readers of this article may identify with the fact that their lives have been anything but smooth. Frequently, the crooked paths and the rough places were their own creation. Conscience tells them that they are the culprits, but they brush it off and look for scapegoats. They look to the left and to the right, and cannot find a way out. They have a deep longing for restoration and wait for it. Sometimes, they make spirited attempts at getting their lives back on track but discover that achieving restoration by the *destroyer* could be very difficult, though not impossible. Like in the history of Jerusalem, we see the handiwork of God's grace in our lives. We see Him turn around things for us, sometimes unexpectedly. In spite of our confusion, we *hear* ourselves saying: *'…Our mouths were filled with laughter,'* – verse 2. Our friends (and even watchers who are not so friendly) cannot but agree with the restoration and say *"The Lord has done great things for them"* – verse 2. If you have not experienced the above situation yet, be assured that it will happen as you pray, do the right things and remain on the watch-out. You will also be able to say *"When the Lord restored the fortunes of Zion, we were like those who dreamed"* – verse 1.

CHAPTER 101

The Arrows of Parents

Psalm 127:1–5

The Bible considers children as the arrows of their parents. By extension, the many children from many parents can be seen as the arrows of the community or entire nation. Seeing or taking children akin to arrows is describing children from an angle different from what is found in Proverbs 22: 6, 15. In this psalm, children are straight but in Proverbs 22, children are malleable. The emphases in this psalm are *direction* and *purpose*. The person with the arrow is the one that takes an aim (direction or trajectory of the journey of the arrow) at the target (purpose). Similarly, parents (and in a wider sense, society) are the ones to show the arrows the way to go; if they do their work well, their children will take the predetermined direction and hit the target. Many people who do not have a purpose in life, and when they find it later, do not achieve the purpose, have the problem because their parents did not do the work or did not know what to do. If you are a parent or planning to be a parent, what do you have in mind for your children? Do you know that if you do not organize your arrows in the quiver (the casing where arrows are stored and carried), some other person will make whatever attempt at that job for you? That person may be unauthorized and totally unqualified.

Interestingly verse 3 states: *'Children are a heritage from the LORD, offspring a reward from him.'* Heritage is *inheritance* and usually the beneficiary does nothing other than to be born into that right; on the other hand, reward is a *prize or payment* and suggests that some degree of work must have been done prior. So, we can surmise that children are both a gift and result of work. How you treat a gift and how you take your work are a reflection of how precious they are to you – the same thing applies to you and your children. God expects *both* parents to tend these young ones up to maturity. Your 'full quiver' does not have to be the same as mine; we all have different capacities. It is only when you have taken good care of your 'arrows' that, as stated in verse 5, *'They will not be put to shame when they contend with their opponents in court.'*

CHAPTER 102

Fruits of Obedience

Psalm 128:1–6

Every fruit-bearing plant produces fruit. Some plants that are in the wild are not primarily fruit-bearing for the benefit of humankind but for birds, wild animals etc. Virtually every endeavor of human beings has some results. These results are what are referred to as 'fruits' in the Word of God. In this passage the precursor of the fruits is obedience. Both obedience and disobedience yield results but disobedience is the subject of another psalm. The passage concentrates on a man's family and the few areas of fruitfulness are: *wife, children and grandchildren.* Every unmarried man who wants commitment (for not all men are interested in commitment), desires to have a wife; every parent prays for children, and every mature couple with adult children expects grandchildren. Sadly, not many give serious thought to what this psalm says in verse 2: *'You will eat the fruit of your labor.'*

Did you realize that there is *labor* in having and keeping a wife, children and grandchildren? Are you willing to be obedient to the directives found in the Bible to make these blessings (fruits) yours? If you and I are selective in obeying God (or, actually disobey Him) in this matter, we will certainly still have results but they will not be blessings. And why would you inadvertently or purposefully go for results that are not desirable? Why should you not be willing and ready to put in the labor required to make your wife a fruitful vine or your children to have the desire to be in the home environment rather than dread it and opt for 'anywhere outside'? And why should you be afraid to stay alive to see your grandchildren as you project into their future, considering the behavior of their fathers and mothers?

I believe you noticed from verses 1 and 4 that the building blocks that will produce the superstructure of satisfaction for you, now and in future, are *obedience* to God's directives in the Bible and *fear* of the Lord. When we run our marriages and homes in obedience and fear of the Lord, blessings follow naturally.

CHAPTER 103

Record of Faults

Psalm 130:1–8

This psalm, in verse 3, tells us: *'If you, LORD, kept a record of sins, Lord, who could stand?'* It is because God does not keep a permanent record of sins that human beings have hope of salvation. It would not have been possible otherwise – and this is because there is no way we could, on our own, change such a record by hook or by crook, as He is not subject to bribery, coercion or any form of intimidation. All people who are born again know this for a fact, and God is waiting for more people to take a step of faith and make this wonderful opportunity of forgiveness and reconciliation by salvation applicable to them. God is willing to welcome sinners, whether they are aged people, middle-aged adults, young people, or children.

The following that the psalmist penned regarding Israel actually applies to whoever would want to come to God and have a Father-child relationship with Him: *'Israel, put your hope in the LORD, for with the LORD is unfailing love and with him is full redemption. He himself will redeem Israel from all their sins'*, verses 7 and 8. Yes, full redemption is within the reach of anyone who would humbly, and in repentance (represented by Godly sorrow and readiness to make a U-turn in life), go to God the Father through Jesus Christ the Son. It does not matter how your record of sins is – actually, no matter how bad your record is, only God knows the real enormity of it; human beings have the characteristic of minimizing their sins and exaggerating the faults of others. It is by His grace and mercy that we are able to receive and enjoy *full redemption* – verse 7.

But having received this redemption and are now enjoying the freedom from carrying the heavy burden of record of our accumulated sins, are we willing to let go of the long list of offenses that people have committed against us? We naturally cannot judge properly; we need not bog ourselves down with such records – this is because where their contents need to be avenged, God does it better than we would ever do.

CHAPTER 104

Caring for The Things of God

Psalm 132: 1–10

With regards to finding a resting place for the Ark of the Covenant – which represented the presence of God with His people, Israel – King David showed so much enthusiasm as this psalm records in verses 2–5. In these verses, King David swore an oath to the Lord, he made a vow to God that he would not enter his house or go to his bed; he would not allow sleep to his eyes or sleepiness to his eyelids, until he found a place for the Lord, a dwelling or residence for the *Mighty One of Jacob*.

David was both a lover of God and a king. He did not behave like you or I who are so wrapped up with our own private matters. These private matters are important but, by the time we are so engrossed in them that we keep God outside our schedules, we are missing the point. It is actually because we have got so used to normality in our lives that many of us take it for granted. Truly, when we wake up in the morning and are able to prepare and dash out of the house or hostel to work or school (and others places of engagement) we, sooner or later, take life and health for granted; we even take our spouses, children, accommodation, employment and position in life, etc. as our right or entitlements. It does not mean that we all must leave what we are doing to become preachers, pastors, evangelists, church workers, etc. primarily. God is the Owner of all things and that includes us and everything we have, are, or hope to be.

God has interests and the interests are supposed to be served by human partners – you and I. We are equipped in various ways to serve the interests of God. It is a privilege, and every child of God should care for the things of God in their own peculiar way. Only David could do what is recorded in this psalm. Is it not frightening that in the particular place where you are, you may be the only person to serve God's interest? How well are you doing it? You and I should go into God's presence, worship Him in humility, and say LORD, come to your resting place (our hearts), and show your great power in and through us, as in verses 7 and 8.

CHAPTER 105

The Lord Honors His People

Psalm 132: 11–18

This chosen passage ends in verse 18 with: *"I will clothe his enemies with shame, but his head will be adorned with a radiant crown."* Honor and glory are attached to certain positions and the Apostle Paul admonished us (and it applies whether we naturally desire to do so or not) in Romans 13: 7 to *'Give to everyone what you owe them: If you owe taxes, pay taxes; if revenue, then revenue; if respect, then respect; if honor, then honor.'* The first part of the verse tends towards government and governing authorities, but respect and honor are dues meant for 'everyone' including parents, teachers, elders, husbands, wives, etc. There are instances that communities and countries give honor to certain selected people; this includes things like Nobel prizes, national honors, etc. These are honors given to individuals, institutions, governments, etc.

There is another type of honor which makes the ones just mentioned pale into insignificance; this is honor from God. Honor from God takes various forms and some of the ones listed in this passage include: Kingdom, *'One of your own descendants I will place on your throne'* (verse 11); Abundance of supplies, *'I will bless her with abundant provisions'* (verse 15); Meeting the needs of the needy in a community or country, *'her poor I will satisfy with food'* (verse 15); Continuous and ever-present direction, *'a lamp for my anointed one'* (verse 17) and Marked out for greatness, *'his head will be adorned with a radiant crown'* (verse 18). It is stated in verse 11 concerning King David: *'The LORD swore an oath to David, a sure oath he will not revoke.'* The same thing applies to God's children today. Whatever God has stated about you in His Word in terms of a covenant relationship, such statements and promises hold true and are immutable. Although you cannot revoke God's plans and desires for you, you may live in ignorance of the facts/truths; or may be satisfied with your status quo, having no intention to make use of the honor He has made available to you. May that not hold true of you, but may you take hold of the honor He has for you.

CHAPTER 106

Desired: Unity in Families

Psalm 133:1–3

In God's plan, the family is intended to be the primary or basic unit of any society. Right from when He decided to provide Adam with Eve as a companion, His desire was that Adam should not be alone or remain forever with Eve; rather, He instructed them to increase in number. The increase from just being a couple to having children and becoming a complete family was right from the drawing board stage. Not many of us today can boast of good reminiscences regarding our families; even fewer can say that they have been encouraged by the examples close by, or the ones they read about. This unfortunate situation is not because the concept of family is impractical, but principally because of the *human factor*. This human factor is not far away but is you and I, and other people who are parents. Even would-be parents are not arming themselves with the tools to have God's recommended family.

Raising a family is similar to having a business partnership. The original intention of a company at the time of incorporation with the relevant government agency is for profitability and success; it is, however, a well-known fact that many registered companies in practice either fail or fall short of their original goals. In the case of a family, the *partnership* is between parents on the one side, and God on the other; for success to be achieved, I dare say that God is the major partner. Sadly, in many families, as you read this, God is treated either as a total stranger or, at best, a 'sleeping partner.' Husbands and wives, parents and children must cease to listen to themselves only and take counsel from their major partner (God).

When we choose to give God the rightful place in the structure and operations of our families, we shall discover *'How good and pleasant it is when God's people live together in unity!'* and be able to testify regarding our families that *'For there the* L<small>ORD</small> *bestows his blessing, even life forevermore',* verses 1 and 3.

CHAPTER 107

Our Sovereign God

Psalm 135:1–7

A sovereign is an entity, e.g. a person, that has supreme power. In modern times the only example of human beings that fit this description are monarchs. But there are fewer monarchies today than there were many years ago. Monarchs are not particularly acceptable to people in contemporary times. This is because in many societies the citizens love freedom and flexibility in conducting their affairs. Reluctance in having sovereigns run the affairs of their countries or nations is also principally because sovereigns are not immune to the many frailties and shortcomings that plague the rest of humankind. It is, therefore, frightening when a community has a selfish, brutal, unfeeling, and reckless person occupying the exalted position of a sovereign; it is worse still when one remembers the fact that sovereigns are not normally deposed, but maintain the office until death parts them from it. The subjects of such monarchs have to bear the brunt of the monarchies until the monarchs are replaced by, hopefully, better and people-friendly monarchs. When a people are blessed with a good sovereign such people rejoice and wish that their monarchy would 'last forever.'

God is the ultimate Sovereign and He is completely different from human sovereigns – the very best of human sovereigns fall short of the sovereignty displayed by God. Verses 5, 6 and 3 of this Psalm tell us that God is not just great but good. *'I know that the L*ORD *is **great***, *that our Lord is greater than all gods. The L*ORD *does whatever pleases him, in the heavens and on the earth,' and also 'Praise the L*ORD*, for the L*ORD *is **good**;'*

What these verses tell us is that God has the innate characteristic of greatness and does not use this it to our disadvantage; rather, He combines it with another quality, i.e. goodness. It is very difficult to find a human being that is great and good; even when you find this rare breed of people, they can only maintain appropriate actions based on a mechanism of checks using sound advisers of like mind. In the case of God, whatever pleases Him is good for us at all times.

CHAPTER 108

Counterfeits Eventually Disappoint

Psalm 135:13–18

Counterfeits and counterfeiting are a reality in life. To have a counterfeit, there must be an original. The original is usually, at a minimum, of good quality. Some originals are peculiar and difficult to fake. Other originals can be counterfeited.

A counterfeit may share similarity with the original in general appearance, shape, size, weight, taste, feeling by touch, labeling and packaging, etc. A counterfeiter would be wasting time to fake an original if they did not have a clear idea what the original is like. They must, to a reasonable extent, have an inkling of the striking qualities or characteristics of what they want to counterfeit. This means that the counterfeiter, though a crook, has to put in significant effort to produce a counterfeit product.

The counterfeits that this passage describes are idols. Idols would receive no attention if they did not reflect the original – God the Creator and Owner of the entire universe. It is very clear that creation reflects the character and nature of God. The problem with idols is that the idolater or the maker of physical idols uses human imagination to create a semblance of God, according to the creative minds of their maker.

Just like other counterfeits (e.g. money in the form of paper or coins, body appearance that is faked or enhanced, food items, jewelry, etc.), these idols simply struggle to **be** what they are not and consequently strive to **do** what they cannot do. Counterfeit material can deceive unwary people some of the time, but they cannot deceive even such people all the time. Certainly, they cannot deceive those who know the original. This is why it is important for every Christian to study God's Word deeply and get well-rooted to avoid being taken in by any form of spiritual counterfeiting.

Counterfeits do not last and they eventually disappoint. When you read verses 15–18 and compare with verses 7–12 you find the marked difference between idols on the one hand, and the God of heaven on the other.

The psalmist says that the maker and the one who trusts in idols shall be like idols. How? They may not be like idols now, but they shall be like them as they will also become unreliable, worthless and unprofitable. The most important thing about idolatry is that those who trust in idols attribute God's rightful worship to them – and there are eternal consequences for that.

CHAPTER 109

God's Love in Creation

Psalm 136:3–9

The portion of Scripture picked for this chapter tells us a little about the love of God, concentrating on His creative acts. Love has as an integral part the interest of its object. This means that when you say you love your brother, sister, father, mother, other family members, friends, colleagues, country, etc. you are stating or implying that you have their best interests at heart.

But is the above always so? Don't we frequently do things without giving any consideration whatsoever to people who are close to us – and we are not referring to those who are distant, and we may never know them? Is it not true that love is a common, but convenient, word that we frequently use when we actually mean lust? The other sad thing is that you may remember that you have been showing love to various people but when it is your turn to receive love you get anything but love. If you find yourself in this situation do not be discouraged but pray to God to help you hold on and depend on Him. You must accept the fact that people will not always reciprocate your love to them.

God is the ultimate in love. 1 John 4: 7 tells us that Love is from God and the next verse pronounces, *'God is love.'* The chosen passage tells us that He showed love in creation by: making the heavens, spreading out the earth on the waters, making the great lights viz. sun, moon and stars. The purposes of these elements of the universe serve wonderful purposes demonstrating God's love. If any of them failed we would all be in trouble.

With respect to us and God's creation, do we really think that we show love to it? You and I may say that we do not have direct access to Neptune, Jupiter and other planetary bodies, but what about the portion of God's creation that we deal with every day – land, rivers, and their teeming creatures? The way we treat God's creation shows that we do not love them, God, or ourselves. Every seemingly little negative act or practice adds to the cumulative damaging effect on God's creation. It is like we deliberately counter God's love for His creation.

CHAPTER 110

We Cannot Hide from God

Psalm 139:7–12

Hiding from (or attempting to hide from) authority is something that most, if not all, of us have done at one time or the other in our lives. This assertion has nothing to do with age, because even toddlers in their normal play revel in the possibility or reality of hiding from their friends, older siblings and parents. From play it becomes reality, as children grow up to find that they are interested in those things that older persons do not approve of. It may not even be what others do not like; we sometimes hide when we are in possession of the things we do not want to share with others. Whether hiding from people is part of fun and entertainment, or because the things we are engaged in could cause us embarrassment if discovered, hiding is practiced by people of all strata of life.

When we extend this hiding matter to our relationship with God, we are taking it to another and higher dimension. The exercise is in futility, simply because we cannot hide from God. It borders on complete lack of knowledge of the nature of God and His capabilities for anyone to think that marital infidelity, child molestation, domestic violence, sexual perversion, cheating at school, corruption in the workplace and in business, occultism, etc. can be hidden from God. It is possible to deceive, confuse or escape from people, but not God.

The psalmist summarized these truths in verses 7–9. He used simple measurements of distance i.e. height, depth and width to explain what he meant. With respect to height, he used the highest location that hiding could take him to – i.e. the heavens, but God is there. He then thought of the deepest places – i.e. the depths of the oceans and seas, but God is there. He reflected on the widths – very few parts of the earth that we can see are as wide as the oceans, yet they are not beyond God's reach. His final concern was darkness, which is the commonest tool for humankind when it comes to hiding; he concluded that with God, there is no difference between darkness and light. The best option is to be open with God for we just cannot hide anything from Him.

CHAPTER III

Freedom from Traps

Psalm 141:1–4, 8–10

When it comes to traps the predator takes pleasure in meticulously setting them; on the flipside the prey uses virtually every available faculty at its disposal to avoid them. In this case what is good for the predator is not good for the prey. Traps are various.

Entrapment is not always physical as it could be social, political, academic, financial, marital, etc. Traps can sometimes be set for self, unawares; at other times, traps meant for another person may act very effectively against the person that set it. This means that young persons may, out of indiscretion, trap themselves in eventual marriages that they ordinarily would not get into if they had given a little thought to the subject, or sought and taken good counsel from people like trusted friends, family, etc. This is an example of setting a trap for self knowingly or unknowingly. When people or prey fall into traps they frequently discover to their chagrin, and usually late, that exiting traps is a different ball game from gaining entry into them. Unfortunately, some traps are such that once the prey is in, there is no exit – ask fish about their experiences with nets and baits.

In spiritual matters we must also be very wise. We should be like this psalmist who knew that he was an enemy to himself almost as much as other people were his enemies. We read in verses 3 and *4 'Set a guard over my mouth, Lord; keep watch over the door of my lips.'* His mouth gave him great concern and he asked for help – God to control the opening of his mouth, in a way similar to a guard that controls entry and exit of people through a manned gate. Our mouths have put us in trouble, haven't they? *'Do not let my heart be drawn to what is evil'* was his next prayer. The heart is a place we should hold with all diligence, but sometimes we still fail; and that is why this prayer is similar to a part of the Lord's Prayer. Finally, we read of external traps: *'Keep me safe from the traps set by evildoers, from the snares they have laid for me'* in verse 9. Part of his survival strategy is found in verse 8 *'But my eyes are fixed on you, Sovereign Lord;'* May we focus on God.

CHAPTER 112

When Abandoned in Despair

Psalm 142:1–7

Despair is not a good state of mind to be in. Despair is a condition of misery and hopelessness. When in despair, joy seems to take flight. Yes, it is a state of mind but something must have happened to push or drag somebody into despair. It is one thing to be in despair and a completely different thing to be abandoned in despair. The normal response by loved ones is to do something to bring hope back to a person in despair. Despair may be consequent upon loss e.g. loss of business through fire, loss of a loved one, loss of paid employment, loss of status or office, etc. Despair may also be one of the results of bad behavior such as gambling or bad decisions like committing funds into questionable *investment* like Ponzi schemes, especially when borrowed money was used to fund them with anticipated quick, positive, returns but things turned amiss. In spite of these examples, it should be clear that despair may or may not have anything to do with what a person did or did not do.

The desire of the person in despair, and the sympathizers, is for that person to get out of it as quickly as possible. What this chapter is about is not the usual. In this case the question arises: What do you do when you are abandoned in despair? The situation is one that the sufferer cannot see a way out. At the same time the people who want to help find it difficult to do so. This passage shows the position that King David found himself in. Verse 4 is part of his prayer in which he told God that there was nobody at his right hand (to help), nobody was concerned for him and absolutely no-one cared for his life. Nobody wants to be there; this is a state of abandonment. But why would there be no human refuge for him? The answer is in verse 6. In this verse the King says that those who pursued him were too strong for him. In that kind of situation who would put oneself on the firing line? It was a situation where it was risky to show close association with King David. Even those who loved him had to stay away for their safety and, perhaps, for their lives. It still happens in our time.

The king had an answer which we would do well to use if we find ourselves in a similar situation and state of mind. The answer was his crying out to God, laying the complaint to Him and asking for mercy – verses 1 and 2. It is *after* God brings deliverance that you will find even the 'righteous' or good people re-appear to associate with a hitherto hopeless person in misery – verse 7. It is when you begin to praise God for your deliverance that you should hope to see people around you. When people desert you, remember that God is nearby to be your Refuge – verse 5. He does not fail.

CHAPTER 113

When God Rules in Our Lives

Psalm 144:9–15

When God rules in the lives of people, or just one person, the Bible tells us in verse 15 of this passage that *'Blessed is the people of whom this is true; blessed is the people whose God is the* LORD.' In the Bible the general or simple understanding of the word *blessed* is that the person is favored by God and is both fortunate and prosperous. It is like being in a country with excellent, exemplary and people-centered leaders, very different from other surrounding countries that have bad, inconsiderate and corrupt leaders. The citizens of this island of goodness should consider themselves fortunate and blessed by God.

Similarly, not many people know the benefits of having God rule their lives. One of the reasons people do not want God to rule their lives through His Son Jesus Christ is that they do not know, or trust, the character of God. They could be suspicious of God and place Him in the same category as the human leaders or rulers who are so unreliable, wicked and selfish. But God is not so. Verse 12 shows that when God is in our lives, our youths (both male and female) will have hope and live sensibly and thus have a proper background for a good future – to their benefits primarily, and to the society generally.

Three benefits are in verses 13 and 14, viz.: (a) Savings that are not depleted, most likely because we shall follow godly ways of living and investment. Many countries and states could learn and ensure good planning with resultant savings in many areas, and avoid mono-economy which is risky; (b) Productivity. In this agrarian society the fields, sheep and oxen were all put into use, just as we should put our youths and elders into productive ventures for themselves and the entire society; and (c) Security. Verse 14 specifically describes absence of insecurity, captivity or anarchy. These evils are the bane of many communities, and a few countries in recent history. Only sadists would not love to have the beautiful scenario painted for us when we – as individuals and various nations – choose to live godly lives. It pays to trust God and have Him rule our lives.

CHAPTER 114

The Lord Is Good to Everybody

Psalm 145:5–11

The part of the passage for this chapter that is chosen for comments is verse 9 which states: *'The LORD is good to all; he has compassion on all he has made.'* From the human perspective, this is awesome and really unnatural for you and me. You and I know that we have the natural tendency to be choosy in allocating our love or applying our goodness. When you watch babies, you will notice that they have a preference for one (or some) of their toys over other toys; they may, without any clear reason, prefer being carried by the grandfather to being carried by the grandmother (or vice versa). As they grow older, children may treat some of their clothes roughly and handle others with care; some children love certain colors and do not like other colors.

Unfortunately, this selective expression of love and goodness sometimes shows itself in much older people, including parents; some parents show preferential love to some of their children. The Bible gives us a very good example of this malady in Genesis where Rebekah loved the younger twin-son Jacob more than Esau. Jacob virtually took over this bad trait and appeared to show more love to Joseph than to his elder sons. It is very difficult to strike a good balance in our relationship with people and our attitude towards things. Thankfully, God is different and He does not have the limitation that human beings have.

God is good to all His creatures and shows compassion to all of us. This goodness covers both living creatures, non-living things, and even the planets; it covers everything. It should be very clear that it is because of God's ability to show a general goodness to humankind (for example) that everyone benefits from His sunshine and rain. It is possible for Him to select but in His goodness, He is inclusive, rather than exclusive. Moreover, God is so good that even people who oppose or dislike him still prosper in life – to the extent that some believe that they lose nothing in keeping God out of their lives. For many watchers it is confusing and the glory of the wicked is described in Psalm 37:1, 35.

The compassion that God has for all people (for all are His creatures) as a result of His goodness, should not be taken for granted by the wicked or those who truly worship Him. For the wicked, they should not be deceived into continuing in their wickedness believing there are no consequences; for true worshippers, they should not relent and begin to eye ungodly ways.

CHAPTER 115

The Where, Why, How and Who of Praise

Psalm 150:1–6

This Psalm, though short, provides the reader with concise information on *the where, why, how and who of praise*. With respect to **'Where'** praises to God should take place, the psalmist gives us the answer as God's sanctuary and His mighty heavens. Sanctuary may not be very clear to every reader but it includes places like your home, children's Sunday school, church auditorium, cathedrals, high (secondary) school assembly halls, meeting halls for Christian students in universities or colleges, etc. Mighty heavens are clearer, as they refer to God's eternal heavens where eternal beings occupy. The **'Why'** consists of God's acts of power and His surpassing or excellent, greatness. As to **'How'** to praise God the Psalm indicates things with which we should praise God. These instruments which give support to the human voice include: trumpet, harp and lyre, tambourine, the entire human body (including dancing), strings and pipe and cymbals. These instruments do not, on their own, produce the sounds of praise but various parts of the human body (principally the mouth and fingers) do the job. These are not all the available instruments as there are many more. Depending on which part of the globe you come from or reside in, you can fill in the list of instruments with the locally available ones. You should feel free to use them to glorify God. Finally, **'Who'** is to praise the Lord?

The writer puts it beautifully thus: 'Everything that has breath'. It is not said 'everybody that has breath'? I believe that it is because 'everything' covers much more than 'everybody' – and includes all manner of animals like flying, walking and creeping things. Various animals praise God in their own peculiar ways. We enjoy the sounds that some of them produce, though the sounds made by others are incomprehensible at best, and annoying at worst. God understands their praises, nevertheless. When you consider all that have breath, we have no excuse not to praise the Lord – and if we do not take our rightful place to do this great service to our great God, other creatures with breath will do it.

Psalm 1:1-6

The Key to Blessings from God

A	M	O	C	K	E	R	S	S	O	U	P	S	R	E	N	N	I	S	W
S	F	A	U	B	L	Q	E	C	P	T	N	E	M	G	D	U	J	F	C
F	Q	S	K	H	T	T	N	E	K	Z	P	A	J	I	W	R	A	V	O
S	R	Z	N	Q	A	E	S	F	H	Y	O	T	Q	O	P	G	P	H	U
C	I	U	B	T	D	S	O	T	T	L	C	H	A	F	F	E	I	T	N
X	W	B	I	W	V	E	A	P	A	C	R	P	E	R	I	S	H	W	S
F	Z	D	M	T	N	A	S	U	E	N	O	A	R	U	T	G	U	F	E
Y	E	C	L	L	F	S	P	R	A	T	D	E	K	C	I	W	M	T	L
M	X	W	P	A	M	O	J	Q	E	V	N	D	A	L	U	Q	B	W	A
J	E	T	E	K	S	N	T	R	C	P	T	K	E	T	C	D	R	Q	S
U	O	L	D	Y	W	Q	O	S	B	W	S	D	Z	E	N	I	G	H	T
S	Y	I	C	R	A	F	G	K	M	S	L	O	X	W	X	F	W	I	R
D	G	T	N	S	E	R	K	L	A	W	O	L	R	G	W	H	Y	G	E
L	O	R	D	R	X	C	U	H	O	H	U	R	M	P	E	J	U	K	A
E	O	J	E	H	S	E	H	C	T	A	W	Q	K	N	Y	O	I	L	M
I	G	H	S	G	V	S	S	J	P	T	N	P	L	A	N	T	E	D	S
Y	T	U	S	F	N	W	K	O	W	E	B	W	J	L	I	P	S	N	I
I	J	L	E	E	O	G	L	W	A	V	G	D	M	C	L	J	R	A	P
P	E	R	L	L	M	P	A	S	S	E	M	B	L	Y	M	I	W	T	L
R	G	T	B	Q	E	L	T	U	G	R	I	G	H	T	E	O	U	S	Z

CLUES

BLESSED   WALK   COUNSEL   STAND
SINNERS   SEAT   MOCKERS   DELIGHT
LAW   LORD   MEDITATES   NIGHT
PLANTED   STREAMS   YIELDS   FRUIT
SEASON   LEAF   WHATEVER   PROSPERS
WICKED   CHAFF   BLOWS   THEREFORE
STAND   JUDGMENT   ASSEMBLY
WATCHES   RIGHTEOUS   PERISH

God Allows Man Authority Over His Creation   **Puzzle 2**

Psalm 8:1-9

G	L	O	R	Y	C	X	H	D	R	E	S	M	Z	A	R	U	L	E	R
G	N	I	H	T	Y	R	E	V	E	B	B	A	V	C	G	K	Y	T	F
W	E	Q	R	T	U	Y	R	I	O	E	P	J	L	H	K	J	R	C	H
D	S	A	D	G	F	H	D	J	K	A	D	E	N	I	A	D	R	O	L
Q	R	W	P	A	T	H	S	E	R	S	T	S	Y	L	U	I	O	N	W
B	Y	O	G	V	F	C	T	R	D	T	D	T	X	D	Z	S	E	S	H
T	Y	U	L	I	O	P	L	N	M	S	K	I	O	R	I	J	N	I	U
L	I	T	T	L	E	Q	A	W	F	E	S	C	R	E	B	I	R	D	S
U	F	A	S	D	F	H	G	I	H	T	J	T	K	N	L	P	O	E	W
F	Q	I	W	E	R	T	E	Y	N	U	I	O	A	P	M	N	B	R	I
D	Z	X	S	C	V	L	B	A	D	E	N	W	O	R	C	S	N	M	M
N	R	G	E	H	D	V	F	T	V	F	C	R	F	D	S	X	E	S	Z
I	U	P	I	L	O	N	K	M	I	E	J	I	N	U	H	C	B	A	Y
M	O	E	M	D	I	C	R	F	V	T	N	G	B	Y	A	H	N	U	S
W	Y	F	E	E	T	E	T	B	Y	G	U	S	I	L	E	N	C	E	I
Z	D	F	N	T	B	W	E	Y	E	I	M	S	P	I	T	J	M	L	C
M	A	V	E	N	G	E	R	R	Q	I	E	X	F	P	H	T	R	A	E
O	D	M	T	E	G	Y	S	U	R	B	N	I	M	S	G	H	R	M	O
O	A	Q	A	W	H	O	N	O	R	E	S	G	T	N	K	E	L	O	F
N	E	A	S	N	C	R	Y	J	N	K	M	N	S	K	C	O	L	F	O

CLUES

MAJESTIC   NAME   EARTH
GLORY   HEAVENS   LIPS   CHILDREN
INFANTS   ORDAINED   SILENCE   FOE
AVENGER   CONSIDER   WORK   FINGERS
MOON   STARS   PLACE   MAN
MINDFUL   SON   CARE   LITTLE
BEINGS   CROWNED   HONOR   RULER
HANDS   EVERYTHING   FEET
FLOCKS   HERDS   BEASTS   FIELD
BIRDS   FISH   SWIM   PATHS
SEAS   LORD   YOUR

Psalm 10:1-13

S	E	I	M	E	N	E	A	Z	S	M	Q	W	Y	S	T	P	A	V	C
Y	F	O	R	G	O	T	T	E	N	X	O	D	E	D	E	R	C	I	O
O	R	F	V	T	T	G	B	Y	E	H	E	U	N	U	R	O	J	C	V
U	S	M	I	K	H	O	L	Y	E	E	P	O	T	O	C	S	L	T	E
R	T	A	S	D	I	F	T	G	R	H	J	K	G	H	E	P	K	I	R
S	R	R	Q	S	N	H	A	G	S	Z	W	A	S	X	S	E	E	M	S
E	E	D	O	C	G	R	F	V	T	G	N	B	Y	H	N	R	U	S	J
L	N	I	K	U	M	N	O	L	P	C	Q	S	A	Z	R	O	O	M	W
F	G	S	A	X	B	E	I	D	E	C	D	R	E	F	V	U	T	G	S
B	T	H	Y	H	N	L	U	V	J	M	E	I	K	S	E	S	R	U	C
V	H	Q	C	A	Z	W	E	S	A	X	V	E	W	S	S	D	C	V	H
I	N	N	O	C	E	N	T	R	F	R	I	I	V	E	T	E	G	B	E
L	Y	E	L	I	V	E	R	H	N	U	C	J	M	L	U	I	L	K	M
L	A	S	L	D	F	G	P	H	T	K	E	T	T	P	C	G	H	B	E
A	Q	N	A	W	E	R	T	N	E	F	S	V	B	L	A	Y	N	H	S
G	Z	E	P	X	I	W	U	D	R	T	G	H	M	E	U	U	N	O	K
E	Z	V	S	D	X	O	V	T	S	H	N	S	T	H	G	U	O	H	T
S	S	E	E	K	C	Q	R	A	G	J	K	L	O	I	H	Y	I	R	E
A	Z	R	D	C	R	B	O	W	R	F	O	R	G	E	T	C	L	N	M
W	R	T	A	A	M	B	U	S	H	Y	H	B	S	T	A	E	R	H	T

CLUES

YOURSELF TROUBLE ARROGANCE WICKED
CAUGHT SCHEMES DEVISES BOASTS
CRAVINGS BLESSES GREEDY PRIDE SEEK
THOUGHTS ROOM PROSPEROUS
HAUGHTY SNEERS ENEMIES NOTHING
MOUTH CURSES THREATS TONGUE
VILLAGES AMBUSH INNOCENT SECRET
LION VICTIMS COLLAPSE
STRENGTH FORGOTTEN COVERS
NEVER FORGET REVILE ACCOUNT

****

QUESTION: In this Puzzle there are six words which appear *slanting* the same way as the word '*ACCOUNT*.' What are these words that God will hold boys and girls, men and women to account? You may choose to check your dictionary or thesaurus for the meaning of each word. **The answers are after Puzzle 10**.

Glory in God's Word and Creation　　　　　　　　　　**Puzzle 4**

Psalm 19:1-14

S	E	S	I	R	A	S	H	D	T	E	N	T	F	G	W	H	J	K	G
Q	V	T	W	E	S	R	A	T	Y	C	O	M	M	A	N	D	S	C	L
U	I	A	I	G	E	O	N	P	L	I	M	K	R	G	O	I	H	O	O
J	G	T	W	O	R	L	D	N	U	O	S	N	O	N	N	P	O	U	R
N	R	U	I	L	V	B	S	H	U	V	E	Y	C	I	S	L	N	R	Y
O	O	T	L	D	A	G	V	D	C	D	F	T	K	H	T	E	E	S	R
I	F	E	L	D	N	E	E	L	X	Z	S	E	W	S	P	A	Y	E	A
P	Q	S	F	W	T	P	A	E	P	R	Y	B	T	E	E	S	C	Y	N
M	U	I	U	O	R	E	P	R	I	H	L	L	K	R	C	I	O	J	O
A	H	G	L	I	V	F	D	S	T	A	T	A	Z	F	E	N	M	X	I
H	E	A	V	E	N	S	H	R	C	H	A	M	B	E	R	G	B	M	S
C	C	E	R	V	B	N	O	M	H	L	K	E	R	R	P	J	H	O	S
G	D	F	E	E	D	W	N	S	E	S	M	L	S	A	A	Q	R	O	E
W	R	E	N	R	T	T	E	Y	D	T	I	E	I	T	W	U	E	R	R
J	O	Y	D	S	N	E	Y	I	H	L	A	S	G	I	O	P	D	G	G
L	L	K	U	I	A	J	E	G	H	U	L	S	H	U	M	W	E	E	S
G	F	R	R	M	I	D	I	W	S	A	C	A	T	C	O	Z	E	D	N
X	T	C	I	P	D	N	V	B	S	F	O	N	M	R	U	Q	M	I	A
W	E	R	N	L	A	T	Y	U	I	O	R	P	D	I	T	L	E	R	R
K	J	H	G	E	R	F	H	C	E	E	P	S	D	C	H	S	R	B	T

CLUES

HEAVENS   GLORY   PROCLAIM   HANDS   POUR
SPEECH   NIGHT   REVEAL   WORDS
SOUND   VOICE   EARTH   WORLD   PITCHED
TENT   BRIDEGROOM   COURSE   RISES
CIRCUIT   DEPRIVED   WARMTH   LORD
REFRESHING   STATUTES   TRUSTWORTHY
SIMPLE   PRECEPTS   JOY   COMMANDS
RADIANT   ENDURING   GOLD   SWEETER
HONEY   HONEYCOMB   SERVANT   WARNED
WILLFUL   BLAMELESS   TRANSGRESSION
MOUTH   PLEASING   SIGHT   ROCK
REDEEMER

Confess and Be Forgiven

Psalm 32:1-7

Q	Y	E	L	B	U	O	R	T	A	Q	F	Q	Y	V	S	Q	Z	B	R
W	U	C	X	Q	D	Z	Z	D	N	U	O	R	R	U	S	W	H	O	T
M	A	N	Z	W	F	F	X	F	S	W	R	A	H	C	D	E	E	N	E
I	I	A	C	K	N	O	W	L	E	D	G	E	D	X	H	C	A	E	R
G	O	R	A	E	G	U	C	D	D	E	I	Z	N	Z	F	R	V	S	O
H	P	E	S	P	H	N	V	S	F	R	V	W	M	A	G	T	Y	J	F
T	A	V	D	T	J	D	B	S	T	R	E	N	G	T	H	Y	X	H	E
Y	S	I	F	E	K	X	N	N	G	T	N	S	J	R	H	U	C	G	R
E	P	L	G	R	L	W	H	O	S	E	H	E	V	A	G	R	O	F	E
S	R	E	T	A	W	C	M	I	H	Y	G	X	U	N	J	Y	V	F	H
O	O	D	H	T	B	L	E	S	S	E	D	C	I	S	P	I	R	I	T
N	T	J	J	Y	M	V	L	S	J	U	E	D	K	G	K	U	B	D	Y
G	E	K	G	U	D	E	R	E	V	O	C	E	L	R	E	M	M	U	S
S	C	L	R	I	N	B	K	R	K	I	E	R	O	E	L	I	N	S	U
R	T	M	O	O	B	N	J	G	L	O	I	F	P	S	I	L	E	N	T
T	D	N	A	G	A	I	N	S	T	P	T	V	M	S	P	O	M	A	I
D	F	B	N	P	V	M	H	N	J	L	F	G	N	I	D	I	H	Q	O
R	G	V	I	D	E	P	P	A	S	K	D	B	N	O	O	P	L	W	P
O	H	C	N	A	C	N	G	R	G	J	S	G	B	N	I	L	K	E	L
L	O	N	G	S	W	A	S	T	E	D	A	T	S	S	E	F	N	O	C

CLUES

TRANSGRESSIONS   FORGIVEN   BLESSED
MAN   LORD   AGAINST   WHOSE SPIRIT
DECEIT   KEPT   SILENT   BONES   WASTED
GROANING   LONG   HEAVY   STRENGTH
SAPPED   SUMMER   ACKNOWLEDGED
CONFESS   TRANSGRESSIONS   FORGAVE
THEREFORE   FOUND   MIGHTY   WATERS
REACH   HIDING   PROTECT   TROUBLE
SURROUND   SONGS   DELIVERANCE

Psalm 37:1-11

V	G	P	Q	O	L	J	A	P	Q	T	S	U	O	E	T	H	G	I	R
W	I	C	K	E	D	N	A	E	A	Y	M	I	D	R	H	Q	U	E	T
A	H	N	A	P	G	O	S	O	Z	W	J	E	U	Z	J	W	H	W	Y
S	J	D	D	E	A	O	D	P	X	I	U	S	F	A	K	T	E	R	F
S	S	A	R	I	S	N	F	L	S	L	T	O	G	A	I	E	I	E	U
U	K	D	W	N	C	D	W	E	L	L	I	H	H	W	S	T	I	L	L
C	L	S	E	H	D	A	G	B	P	H	K	T	J	A	L	S	O	I	A
C	Q	F	R	E	F	Y	T	V	W	O	L	U	K	Y	P	U	P	K	N
E	H	T	A	R	W	K	H	I	E	N	H	I	L	S	O	R	L	E	D
E	W	G	T	I	G	E	N	J	O	Y	P	O	M	D	I	T	K	R	I
D	E	H	Y	T	T	L	J	C	E	N	V	I	O	U	S	R	E	P	O
F	R	J	M	L	I	M	K	R	E	F	R	A	I	N	U	D	H	R	P
P	T	K	E	K	M	N	L	S	D	S	Q	P	N	F	E	T	G	O	F
L	I	V	E	J	M	B	U	X	E	E	W	L	B	Y	Y	R	G	S	O
A	Y	L	K	H	O	A	M	M	C	R	E	O	O	G	A	Y	F	P	U
N	U	M	U	G	C	V	E	A	V	U	R	R	V	S	T	H	D	E	N
T	D	E	L	I	G	H	T	Q	B	T	T	D	S	H	R	E	S	R	D
S	A	N	B	F	C	C	E	F	A	S	T	A	C	I	E	A	A	I	Q
D	I	K	I	S	H	X	N	D	E	A	Y	S	X	N	W	R	Q	T	A
F	O	S	E	R	I	S	E	D	G	P	A	T	I	E	N	T	L	Y	Z

CLUES

FRET   BECAUSE   EVIL   ENVIOUS   LIKE
GRASS   WITHER   PLANTS   WILL   AWAY
TRUST   LORD   DWELL   SAFE   PASTURE
TAKE   DESIRES   HEART   COMMIT
TRUST   RIGHTEOUS   SHINE   VINDICATION
NOONDAY   STILL   PATIENTLY   PEOPLE
SUCCEED   SCHEMES   REFRAIN   ANGER
WRATH   LEADS   DESTROYED   THOSE
HOPE   LAND   WICKED   FOUND
MEEK   INHERIT   ENJOY   PROSPERITY

Wanted: Excellent Kings, Inside and Out　　　　　　　　　　**Puzzle 7**

Psalm 45: 1 – 8

X	R	M	I	G	H	T	Y	Z	V	K	I	N	G	Q	X	N	Z	W	J
E	F	S	Z	M	P	F	T	C	T	H	G	N	I	T	N	I	O	N	A
C	G	R	I	G	H	T	I	X	N	J	K	U	F	O	R	E	V	E	R
I	H	D	X	J	H	V	L	V	E	K	M	Y	R	R	H	B	D	E	E
T	J	J	C	R	O	D	I	H	L	U	F	L	L	I	K	S	E	T	T
S	O	F	O	Y	I	O	M	T	L	R	J	T	K	W	C	D	T	U	P
U	F	N	V	Y	I	G	U	U	E	V	F	R	A	G	R	A	N	T	E
J	E	G	G	T	U	D	H	R	C	I	F	F	R	E	Y	W	I	L	C
D	C	H	B	U	Y	G	M	T	X	C	O	M	P	A	N	I	O	N	S
S	D	E	S	S	E	L	B	B	E	T	D	S	T	R	I	C	N	G	O
E	N	J	N	R	T	A	W	E	S	O	M	E	U	G	W	K	A	B	K
O	I	S	E	C	A	L	A	P	F	R	U	G	F	T	H	E	M	E	I
L	O	K	Y	E	T	H	H	M	G	I	S	S	X	K	G	D	V	N	N
A	R	R	O	W	S	K	F	K	L	O	S	T	N	T	J	N	M	E	G
F	Y	L	U	W	T	M	D	O	A	U	C	I	D	E	D	E	A	M	D
N	R	P	R	Q	R	U	E	I	D	S	Y	R	N	C	S	S	I	I	O
D	O	O	S	D	I	S	O	Y	C	L	I	R	M	A	K	S	S	E	M
F	D	B	E	G	N	I	V	O	R	Y	O	E	D	R	O	W	S	S	N
G	C	U	L	H	G	C	P	R	Z	W	L	D	L	G	I	P	A	O	T
T	E	E	F	E	S	U	A	D	O	R	N	E	D	L	L	Q	C	E	E

CLUES

STIRRED   NOBLE   THEME   KING   TONGUE
SKILLFUL   EXCELLENT   ANOINTED   GRACE
BLESSED   FOREVER   SWORD   MIGHTY
YOURSELF   VICTORIOUSLY   TRUTH   HUMILITY
JUSTICE   RIGHT   AWESOME   ARROWS
ENEMIES   FEET   THRONE   SCEPTER
KINGDOM   RIGHTEOUSNESS   WICKEDNESS
GOD   COMPANIONS   ANOINTING   OIL
JOY   FRAGRANT   MYRRH   ALOES   CASSIA
PALACES   ADORNED   IVORY
MUSIC   STRINGS   GLAD

How to Handle Fear

Psalm 56: 1 – 13

F	E	E	T	M	L	R	T	J	L	K	M	P	I	M	Q	M	D	W	Z
G	M	P	Q	N	U	P	G	T	J	P	I	R	G	O	S	S	E	R	P
F	N	U	S	I	F	O	H	R	H	R	S	I	N	R	E	G	A	Q	X
D	B	R	N	B	I	I	K	U	G	A	E	D	I	T	L	N	T	R	S
S	V	S	E	V	C	O	N	S	P	I	R	E	K	A	L	I	H	T	F
A	T	U	T	C	R	U	T	T	F	S	Y	Z	C	L	O	R	V	Y	Q
S	N	I	T	U	E	Y	R	L	S	E	I	R	A	S	R	E	V	D	A
T	E	T	H	X	M	T	E	K	E	S	K	X	T	W	C	F	C	E	T
E	S	U	A	C	E	B	W	J	I	A	J	N	T	R	S	F	D	L	T
P	E	X	J	Z	Z	R	L	W	M	F	G	A	A	D	A	O	S	I	A
S	R	C	K	X	S	E	S	I	E	G	T	T	O	H	S	N	G	V	C
Q	P	V	L	V	W	R	D	C	N	S	W	I	P	I	L	B	H	E	K
U	N	D	E	R	R	E	V	K	E	G	I	O	T	O	U	E	J	R	T
W	C	Z	A	N	S	C	H	E	M	E	S	N	P	U	R	S	U	E	Y
R	R	X	S	M	F	O	B	D	F	H	T	S	E	A	K	C	T	D	G
T	X	E	D	G	B	R	N	N	I	J	F	C	W	Z	F	A	E	O	H
H	Z	B	G	H	V	D	F	E	S	A	D	V	V	H	O	P	I	N	G
G	S	N	F	N	N	W	C	S	S	K	R	B	S	R	A	E	T	P	N
I	O	M	G	D	A	Q	M	S	R	B	E	F	O	R	E	V	U	H	O
L	I	F	E	X	T	Y	A	K	E	L	S	W	A	T	C	H	O	F	L

CLUES

MERCIFUL   ENEMIES   PURSUIT   LONG
PRESS   ATTACK   ADVERSARIES   PURSUE
LONG   PRIDE   ATTACKING   AFRAID
TRUST   MORTALS   TWIST   SCHEMES
RUIN   CONSPIRE   LURK   WATCH   STEPS
HOPING   TAKE   BECAUSE   WICKEDNESS
ESCAPE   ANGER   NATIONS   RECORD
MISERY   TEARS   SCROLL   PRAISE   UNDER
PRESENT   OFFERINGS   DELIVERED   DEATH
FEET   STUMBLING   BEFORE   LIGHT   LIFE

God Cares for Our Environment; So, Should I

Psalm 65:5-13

A	Y	G	S	D	N	A	L	S	S	A	R	G	D	K	S	O	N	G	S
N	U	B	R	F	R	Z	A	R	J	C	A	R	S	J	T	U	A	R	G
S	A	O	T	D	E	X	N	E	H	V	H	T	A	H	R	F	S	I	E
W	R	U	Y	S	V	C	D	D	G	B	C	Y	Q	S	E	A	S	G	N
E	M	N	U	A	E	V	H	N	F	N	N	U	W	R	A	R	D	H	R
R	E	T	A	W	N	S	W	O	D	A	E	M	E	E	M	T	F	T	I
Q	D	Y	I	Q	I	E	G	W	F	U	R	R	O	W	S	H	G	E	C
W	I	F	O	W	N	G	F	U	D	M	D	I	R	O	W	E	P	O	H
E	O	D	P	H	G	D	D	C	R	O	W	N	T	H	E	S	H	U	F
R	P	S	L	I	T	I	S	A	S	L	Q	O	Y	S	R	T	J	S	D
S	K	C	O	L	F	R	A	R	A	C	A	R	E	G	T	I	K	B	S
A	L	A	K	L	Y	B	Q	T	Z	K	W	P	U	F	Y	O	L	N	A
W	A	V	E	S	U	N	W	S	X	J	E	C	N	A	D	N	U	B	A
E	K	Q	J	E	I	M	E	I	V	H	E	L	I	D	M	P	Z	M	Q
S	T	I	L	L	E	D	R	O	A	G	D	K	C	L	O	T	H	E	D
O	J	W	H	H	O	L	T	P	L	F	E	J	O	S	R	L	X	L	W
M	O	U	N	T	A	I	N	S	L	F	M	H	M	A	N	T	L	E	D
E	H	E	H	R	P	K	Y	L	E	D	R	G	P	A	I	K	C	J	E
T	G	R	G	A	L	J	U	K	Y	R	O	A	R	I	N	G	V	H	R
W	I	L	D	E	R	N	E	S	S	S	F	F	L	Q	G	R	A	I	N

CLUES

ANSWER   AWESOME   RIGHTEOUS   HOPE
EARTH   FARTHEST   FORMED   MOUNTAINS
STILLED   ROARING   WAVES   WONDERS
MORNING   EVENING   SONGS   CARE
LAND   WATER   ENRICH   ABUNDANTLY
STREAMS   DRENCH   FURROWS   RIDGES
SHOWERS   CROWN   BOUNTY   CARTS
ABUNDANCE   GRASSLANDS   WILDERNESS
HILLS   CLOTHED   MEADOWS
FLOCKS   VALLEYS   MANTLED   GRAIN

Understand When Others Don't!   Puzzle 10

Psalm 71:9–17

A	G	O	D	J	R	E	S	C	U	E	Y	Z	B	E	M	A	H	S	W
C	M	O	R	F	Y	C	O	M	E	P	Z	Y	O	U	T	H	Q	P	E
Q	S	N	Y	W	O	N	K	S	P	A	C	C	U	S	E	R	S	K	E
U	E	G	U	R	V	R	U	O	Y	J	E	C	A	R	G	S	I	D	P
I	V	T	N	A	W	B	S	P	E	A	K	F	E	U	L	O	W	T	O
C	A	S	T	R	F	Y	F	A	L	L	F	H	N	P	E	R	I	S	H
K	H	S	T	C	A	N	U	S	K	E	T	O	G	O	N	E	A	L	I
L	D	U	R	W	A	I	T	T	Y	E	E	S	E	I	M	E	N	E	P
Y	F	A	L	O	N	E	P	M	G	E	N	K	Y	Z	L	L	I	K	T
F	E	A	W	I	U	T	H	O	U	G	H	G	S	X	R	T	J	A	M
W	R	S	Y	T	I	E	T	U	O	N	G	I	E	R	E	V	O	S	I
T	A	U	G	H	T	S	Y	T	H	E	M	B	I	F	I	C	U	R	A
E	L	O	I	O	P	H	X	H	E	L	P	D	Z	H	T	O	N	O	L
A	C	E	J	S	S	F	L	O	R	D	U	A	E	E	L	N	R	F	C
G	E	T	S	E	A	M	L	O	R	M	D	Y	M	E	S	S	E	T	O
A	D	H	I	P	V	I	E	I	N	Y	O	D	V	X	W	P	T	E	R
I	H	G	N	L	I	G	T	T	U	G	W	R	D	E	S	I	A	R	P
N	K	I	C	Y	N	H	B	Y	A	W	A	J	E	K	I	R	L	W	B
S	T	R	E	N	G	T	H	U	P	M	R	A	H	I	D	E	E	D	S
T	N	F	A	R	B	Y	O	U	R	S	Y	M	C	O	V	E	R	E	D

CLUES

CAST AWAY FORSAKE STRENGTH GONE
ENEMIES SPEAK AGAINST THOSE WAIT
KILL CONSPIRE TOGETHER FORSAKEN
PURSUE SEIZE RESCUE FAR FROM
GOD COME QUICKLY HELP ACCUSERS
PERISH SHAME WANT HARM COVERED
SCORN DISGRACE ALWAYS HOPE
PRAISE MORE MOUTH TELL YOUR
RIGHTEOUS SAVING LONG THOUGH
KNOW RELATE THEM MIGHTY
ACTS SOVEREIGN LORD PROCLAIM
DEEDS YOURS ALONE SINCE YOUTH
HAVE TAUGHT DAY DECLARE
MARVELOUS

ANSWER TO QUESTION

The six words are:

HAUGHTY

GREEDY

ARROGANCE

PRIDE

WICKED

BOASTS

ABOUT THE AUTHOR

Inyang UKOT has a passion for personal and family growth among Christians. He is fully persuaded that every part of the Bible is relevant to the modern world and our daily living; a little study, even in a relaxed mood like engaging the mind by playing puzzles, is at least one step forward in achieving the desired positive experience with God and fellow humankind. At the time of this publication he has been in continuous practice as a physician for 38 years; he has two post-graduate fellowships in Family Medicine dated 28 and 24 years respectively. He also has a post-graduate diploma of the Royal College of Physicians of London, in Occupational Medicine. He is married to Sarah and has four adult daughters: Grace, Elor, Sarah Jr. and Joy.

Printed in the United States
By Bookmasters